"Dreams are God's coded language revealed to chosen individuals for strategic action in kairos moments. May this book refresh you!"

Dr. Emmanuel Ziga, president and founder of Grace For All
Nations Ministries International

"Dreams are one of the most significant ways the Lord speaks to us to bring clear and supernatural revelation. You see, if the God of the universe doesn't sleep, then His revelation to us doesn't sleep. In your hands is a great resource to awaken, activate, and empower your dream life to hear His voice supernaturally and effectively. Thank you, Demontae, for this anointed, empowering, and practical teaching for such a time as this!"

Rebecca Greenwood, co-founder of Christian Harvest
International Strategic Prayer Apostolic Network

The
SUPERNATURAL
DIMENSION
of
DREAMS

UNDERSTANDING HOW
GOD WORKS
WHILE YOU SLEEP

DEMONTAE A. EDMONDS

Chosen

a division of Baker Publishing Group
Minneapolis, Minnesota

Published by Chosen Books
Minneapolis, Minnesota
www.chosenbooks.com

Chosen Books is a division of
Baker Publishing Group, Grand Rapids, Michigan

Printed in the United States of America

ISBN 978-0-8007-6346-6 (trade paper)
ISBN 978-1-4934-4235-5 (ebook)
ISBN 978-0-8007-3001-7 (casebound)

Library of Congress Control Number: 2023026467

Baker Publishing Group publications use paper produced from sustainable forestry practices and post-consumer waste whenever possible.

23 24 25 26 27 28 29   7 6 5 4 3 2 1

This book is dedicated to the dreamers all around the world. The man in Africa who is dreaming about new ways to farm and improve agriculture in his community. The woman in Asia who is dreaming about a cure for breast cancer. The man in Hollywood who is dreaming about a new television series that will encourage young people not to conform to the peer pressures of society. The little girl in South America who is dreaming of being the first female leader of her nation, and will help improve democracy. The little boy in Europe who is dreaming about starting a tuition-free private school for refugees coming into Europe from North Africa and the Middle East. The person in Australia who is dreaming about building cities of the future in the Australian desert. The prince in Dubai who is dreaming about new ways to improve energy efficiency and provide new energy sources for the world. This book is dedicated to you all, and to all the others like you.

This book is especially dedicated to all of us
who are dreaming about the many ways that we can
share the Gospel of the Lord Jesus Christ.

Contents

Introduction: Dreams Are Treasure Chests   15
Besides detailing the purpose and scope of this book, this introduction will give you a sense of how God can use dreams as a divine conduit to share supernatural insights with us. In fact, He has used the human vehicle of dreams throughout history to communicate with those who are listening. Dreaming is an adventure; one dream from God can change your life!

1. How to Remember Your Dreams   21
In this chapter, I will discuss practical things you can do to help remember your dreams. Being able to remember your dreams is an important skill that will help you gain a greater understanding of what God is attempting to reveal to you through dreams. You will also learn how to record and archive your dreams for future reference.

2. Activate Your Dream Life Now   33
In this chapter, you will receive keys to activate and increase your communication with God via dreams. We will also discuss spiritual factors and soulish issues that can affect the frequency and depth of our dreams. Dreaming may have been a struggle in the past for you, but after applying the instructions in this chapter, expect for your dream life to ascend into a new dimension.

3. What Happens When We Sleep 45

In this chapter, we will discuss the physiological purposes of sleep. We will also talk about the biochemical processes that take place during sleep and the four stages of sleep. Finally, we will discuss how although sleep is a natural process, God has the ability to make it a supernatural experience. The supernatural is just God's super placed on top of our natural! All of this provides a foundation that will serve as a segue into a deeper exploration of how God speaks in the night.

4. Dream but Discern 55

In this chapter, you will learn how your own soul and subconscious can be the source of certain dreams. We will look at "soulish dreams" that are not from the spirit realm (good or bad), but that come from our own experiences. Some such dreams might be "pizza dreams," since food can affect our dream life, or they might be dreams that come from things that have entered our eye and ear gates, which is why it's so important to monitor what we allow in. Soulish dreams can occasionally have some value, but dreams from God are far better.

5. Those Bad Dreams 67

In this chapter, we will discuss the source of bad dreams, and some reasons why and how nightmares occur. We will also talk about the activity of demonic spirits that can influence negative and tormenting dreams. I will also give instructions on how to prevent and counter these types of dreams and their impact on your life.

6. The God Kind of Dreams 81

In this chapter, I will talk about the elements and commonalities of dreams that come from God. Dreams can emanate from a variety of sources, but the ones that proceed from Him are the most important. Learning how to discern "the God kind of dreams" is vital to our spiritual walk and to experiencing victory. We will look at seven rules of thumb for this that will help you achieve success in identifying dreams that come from God.

7. The Dream Compass 97

In this chapter, we will focus on the nature and ability of God to give instructions and directions through dreams. I'll give you both biblical and modern-day examples of how God helped individuals make the right choices through divine inspiration and revelation during sleep. We will also look at how, through dreams, God gives us answers to questions we have proposed in prayer. I'll share one personal account about how God opened a supernatural door to the nation of Ireland through a dream revelation. Another account will be about how God

Contents

Twenty Questions & Answers about Supernatural Dreams 155

In this Q&A section, I will address some of the questions you may be asking after reading this book. These will be some of the most common questions that individuals ask concerning dreams. Also, this section can serve later as a quick reference for you, if you find yourself in a situation where you have the opportunity to answer other people's questions about relating to God through dreams.

Acknowledgments 171

Notes 173

Foreword

When I was eighteen, I had my first dream in which I recognized God was speaking to me. I was away at Bible college when I dreamed my younger brother got very sick and died. When I awakened from the dream, I had tears rolling down my face, wetting my pillow. It took me a moment to realize that what I had experienced was just a dream, because it all seemed so real. So I lay in bed and began to console myself with the words parents teach their children when they have had dreams: *It was just a dream, it was just a dream.*

Suddenly, I heard the Spirit of the Lord say, "No! It is not just a dream! Get up and pray!" So I quickly got up and began to walk back and forth in my dorm room, crying out for the life of my brother. After a while, I felt a peace and returned to bed.

The next morning, my mother called from another state. She said, "I am so glad I caught you. I need to tell you what happened to your brother last night. He was on a deep woods camping trip when his appendix ruptured. By the time his buddies carried him in from the woods and drove him to the hospital, he almost died. Doctors say he is very fortunate."

I realized God had spoken to me in a dream to alert me to intercede for my brother's life. I knew absolutely nothing about dreams. When I was a teenager, no one was talking about God speaking, let alone speaking in dreams. I thought perhaps this was one of those strange, once-in-a-lifetime experiences that can only be explained as supernatural.

But two years later, I had a similar dream about the life of that same brother. This time I dreamed he was driving his car on his way to school. As he came through an intersection, someone failed to stop at the red light and hit my brother's car on the driver's side with such force it rolled over three times and was completely crushed. In my dream, my brother was killed instantly.

When I awakened from this dream, I once again had tears rolling down my face. But because of my previous dream, I immediately got out of bed and began to pray for my brother.

The next morning, my brother was on his way to school when another driver failed to stop at a red light. Their vehicle struck my brother's on the driver's side so hard it rolled over three times and was completely crushed. But the difference was my brother walked out of the car without even a scratch on his body.

Wow! It made me begin to wonder how many other times God had tried to speak to me in a dream and I was unaware. Lives could be hanging in the balance. I needed to learn to hear God's voice in the dimension of dreams.

I embarked on a journey of studying the Scripture on the subject of dreams and visions. I found there were over fifty instances in which God communicated His heart, will, and mind to humankind through a dream or a vision. God birthed the nation of Israel out of an encounter with Abraham in a vision and dream. God promoted Joseph to the prime minister of Egypt because of two dreams of Joseph and two dreams of Pharaoh. Solomon became the wisest man that ever lived because of an impartation from God in a dream. Peter answered the call to the

Gentiles because of a series of visions on a rooftop in Joppa. Paul redirected his missionary journeys because of a vision in which a man from Macedonia called to him for help. Scripture is filled with God's encounters through dreams and visions that changed the course of history.

Acts 2:15–18 tells us of the power of the outpouring of the Holy Spirit. God promised He would pour His Spirit out on all flesh and the result would be, "Your sons and your daughters shall prophesy, your young men shall see visions, your old men shall dream dreams." When our lives are filled with the Holy Spirit, we are given access to the supernatural dimension of revelation, including prophecy, dreams, and visions. It should be a normal part of the life of every believer to hear the voice of the Lord in dreams.

I was honored to write one of the earliest books on this subject. *Dreams and Visions* has been a bestseller on the subject for many years.

But I am very excited about this new book by my friend Demontae Edmonds, which brings a fresh approach to the subject. Demontae carries a strong prophetic anointing and has a great depth of personal experience with hearing God's voice, as well as the ability to teach others the vital skill of dream interpretation. This book will challenge you to press into a deeper intimate relationship with the Lord and begin to tune your ear to the supernatural realm as never before. As you read, you will receive greater revelation and a powerful impartation of prophetic anointing in your life. Your dream life will never be the same.

Jane Hamon, author, *Dreams and Visions*, *The Cyrus Decree*, *The Deborah Company*, *Discernment*, and *Declarations for Breakthrough*

Introduction

Dreams Are Treasure Chests

For some people, hearing or reading about dreams invokes feelings of fear or anxiety. But for most of us, the discussion of dreams is an exciting and adventurous topic. There is so much we can learn about life, our surroundings, and our past, present, and future through dreams. Dreams allow us insight into the windows of our own soul and also into the mind of God. I wrote this book because I'm convinced that dreams should be valued, appreciated, and investigated.

Sleeping may not seem like an exciting venture, but after reading this book, you will have a divine expectancy of what God can do not only while you are awake, but even as you sleep. God has created dreams as a divine conduit for His supernatural communication of wisdom, favor, instruction, correction, warning, and much more! One dream from God has the innate ability to shift you onto a new path of victory. A dream from God can open your eyes to see the plans of the enemy and to overcome them by the wisdom of heaven.

Dreams may not seem as sensational or dramatic as heavenly encounters or angelic visitations, but they are often just as profound and life changing. They are just as *supernatural*. The Bible says in Psalm 121:4, "He who keeps Israel shall neither slumber nor sleep." God does not work "bankers' hours." God's job of masterfully orchestrating the affairs of the universe and our lives is nonstop. While we're sleeping, God is still working on our behalf.

In every generation since the beginning of time, I believe that humankind has been dramatically impacted by the powerful imagery of dreams. Also, God has used the human vehicle of dreams to communicate concepts, warnings, and new ideas to societies throughout history. Throughout time, individuals who were cultural influencers and historical figures such as Socrates, Pontius Pilate's wife, Abraham Lincoln, and Nikola Tesla were all inspired at some point by dreams.

Niels Bohr, father of the physics discipline of quantum mechanics, credits a dream with helping him with the revelation of the atom and its components, such as its nucleus. Many other great scientists, business leaders, and medical experts have also shared how dreams have helped them with discoveries, innovations, and the ability to solve complex issues. There is a well-known dream relating to Albert Einstein's theory of relativity and his understanding of the speed of light. In the dream, Einstein saw himself running down a mountain, chasing after a beam of light. As he moved faster, his surroundings distorted. This dream, which amazingly he had at the age of sixteen, helped him years later with his theoretical comprehension.

The word *Google* has become synonymous with information and the internet. "Google it" is a common term we all use when someone asks a question and we are uncertain of the answer, or when we need to find information quickly on a topic. However, many of us are not aware that the idea for Google came to the company's co-founder, Larry Page, through a divinely inspired dream. In a 2009 commencement address at the University of Michigan, he shared the story of his dream:

> You know what it's like to wake up in the middle of the night with a vivid dream? And you know how, if you don't have a pencil and pad by the bed to write it down, it will be completely gone the next morning?
>
> Well, I had one of those dreams when I was 23. When I suddenly woke up, I was thinking, *What if we could download the whole web, and just keep the links, and* . . . I grabbed a pen and started writing! Sometimes it is important to wake up and stop dreaming. I spent the middle of that night scribbling out the details and convincing myself it would work. Soon after, I told my advisor, Terry Winograd, it would take a couple of weeks to download the web—he nodded knowingly, fully aware it would take much longer but wise enough to not tell me. The optimism of youth is often underrated! Amazingly, I had no thought of building a search engine. The idea wasn't even on the radar. But much later, we happened upon a better way of ranking webpages to make a really great search engine, and Google was born. When a really great dream shows up, grab it![1]

It can be said that the mystery of the atom, Einstein's theories, and Google have all changed the way we understand and do life. Since these concepts were all impacted or inspired by dreams, it can also be said that dreams—especially those from God—have changed the course of human history. How exciting! You may not be a PhD graduate from Harvard University or a Rhodes Scholar, yet we all have the God-given capacity to receive supernatural dreams. This truth should excite you!

My own journey with supernatural dreams began when I was a young boy. Ever since I could remember, I was a dreamer of dreams. Because I dreamed so frequently for years, it didn't take me long to discern between the dreams that were from my own heart and those that were from God. I quickly learned that the ones from God were the most revealing and thrilling.

Some of the supernatural dreams I've experienced have been so graphic and intense that they felt as if I were living through an action movie. Many people have reported to me that they have had dreams that seem catastrophic or apocalyptic in nature. The reason for these dreams is often easily explained once a person understands how and why God may send dreams of this nature. In contrast, the majority of dreams are positive, upbeat, and have helped build my faith.

Dreams have become an integral part of my spiritual life. Where many people may feel some anxiety about dreams, I feel anxiety when I go too long without dreaming. Consider a supernatural dream that God gives you as a secret treasure chest of revelation. Those who have grown to value their dreams also grow in excavating the rich treasures hidden within each dream. I can literally say that more than once, a supernatural dream has saved my life or the life of one of my family members. You will read about some of these powerful testimonies later in this book.

I didn't realize that God was preparing me to help others discover and understand their own dreams for years, until I had experienced several hundred dreams of my own. Now, I often advise people to create a dream journal. The root word in the word *journal* is *journey*. Our dream life can become an exciting and engaging journey. Whether I am talking with a street person who is being warned by God to leave a life of criminal activity, or with the leader of a nation who is trying to decipher the wisdom of God found within his or her dream, or with a single mom who is just trying to "figure life out," it's always a humbling and privileged feeling for me to help others uncover what God may be speaking to them through their dreams.

It has been my prayer and hope to help even more individuals discover the purpose and power of their dreams. Writing

The Supernatural Dimension of Dreams is an answer to that prayer. Contained within each chapter is practical yet revelatory information, along with real-life accounts, to help dreamers gain a greater comprehension of the supernatural dream realm.

Humankind was created to be in an intimate relationship with God. Since the days of Adam and Eve, God has desired to interact with His greatest creation. Genesis 3:8 tells us of Adam and Eve: "And they heard the sound of the LORD God walking in the garden in the cool of the day." If we perceive properly, we can hear God's voice as we sleep. Supernatural dreams not only help convince us that God is speaking to us in the night and working on our behalf, but also help convince us that we are His children.

I believe we are entering into an era of unprecedented supernatural and prophetic grace—a time that the prophets of old prophesied and longed to experience. In Matthew 13:17, Jesus says, "For assuredly, I say to you that many prophets and righteous men desired to see what you see, and did not see it, and to hear what you hear, and did not hear it." Today, an outpouring of supernatural dreams and visions is more important than ever in communicating the heartbeat of God to us. Supernatural dreams in this hour will help us become perfectly aligned with God's empowerment, will, timing, and eternal purposes.

This book's practical insights and biblical foundation will give you a deeper understanding of how God works through dreams to communicate His heart and mind. Each chapter discusses a different principle that will help you comprehend what is taking place in your dreams and how to properly respond to it. I believe that as you read this book, your faith for greater destiny-shifting dreams will increase. Lives have been shaped due to dreams! Destinies have been shifted due to dreams! God has made Himself known through dreams! I'm excited for you to explore all of this with me as you read *The Supernatural Dimension of Dreams: Understanding How God Works While You Sleep.*

one

How to Remember
Your Dreams

The major challenge many people express in relation to understanding their dreams is the first hurdle of being able to remember their dreams in the first place. Without being able to remember your dream, there is little hope of receiving further insight into what God is attempting to reveal during your time of sleep.

Remembering my dreams was a previous challenge for me as well. However, God has given me some practical keys to help me become more efficient at dream recollection. In this chapter, I want to share some of these pointers with you.

A Mindset of Expectancy

The first key I teach people to help them remember their dreams is to have a mindset of expectancy. The *Merriam-Webster* defines *expect* as "to anticipate or look forward to the coming or occurrence of" something.[1] Expect God to reveal things to you in dreams, and expect your spirit to pick up on spiritual activity. Many people fail to recall their dreams because they have little expectation that they will dream at all. Develop an attitude that causes your mind to anticipate and desire to remember your dreams.

There have been times that nondreamers have expressed to me a desire to dream more, as well as dreamers who have simply fared poorly in remembering their dreams. My first goal with these individuals is always to coach them into first believing that God desires for them to dream, and that dreaming should be part of their human experience. My second admonishment is that they must start believing they will dream and remember what they dreamed.

As I changed my own mindset and increased the value I placed on my dream life, my subconscious almost automatically began to recall dreams upon my awakening in the morning hours. Fleeting dreams have become fewer and fewer. My ability to recall the details within my dreams has also drastically increased. Remember, this first key is all mental! Like me, you will experience success in recollecting your dreams as you apply this first key and the others I will share with you.

Bedside Tools

Another key I teach is having bedside tools readily available. One of the easiest and most practical ways to remember your dreams is to keep a notepad and pencil or pen by your bedside. As soon as you awaken, make an active attempt to recollect any dreams or messages that God may have given you in the night. Immediately begin to write down whatever you remember. Sometimes you may only remember a fleeting thought or a portion of your dream, but as you begin to write it down, more and more details may start to come into your conscious memory.

22

Many of us lead very busy lives, and from the moment we awaken, a hectic day starts. You may feel too much in a rush in the mornings to write out an entire dream, but I have learned some shortcuts. When writing down your dream on a notepad, instead of taking time to write out the entire dream, simply write out a few key words that summarize the dream. For instance, if I had a dream about an angel floating on a cloud, who handed me a golden key, I would write *angel, gold key,* and *cloud* in my journal. Later in the day, I would type or write out the entirety of the dream, using those key words as guide markers to remember the entire dream's content.

Another timesaving method for journaling your dreams is to use a recording device instead of pen and paper. A digital recorder or voice recording app saves time and allows you to verbalize your dream quickly and save it in an audio file. Most individuals will not need to purchase a separate digital recorder for this, as many smartphones have voice recording capabilities that allow similar functionality. Another advantage of using this method is that you can download important dreams onto a computer or external hard drive, and then into an archive for later reference.

In the past when I have experienced difficulty journaling my dreams, I have stood on a promise of Jesus found in John 14:26 (KJV): "But the Comforter, which is the Holy Ghost, whom the Father will send in my name, he shall teach you all things, and bring all things to your remembrance, whatsoever I have said unto you." I exercised my faith in this Scripture by praying, *Lord Jesus, I know that you spoke to me in the night. You promised that your Holy Spirit would bring back into my memory what you have revealed. Please, Holy Spirit, help me now remember my dreams.* Amazingly, many times God has been faithful to bring back all the details of a dream that I could barely remember before praying this prayer.

As you journal your dreams each morning, you will discover that this exercise will often cause the understanding or

23

interpretation of a dream to be unlocked for you. Just as important as remembering a dream is understanding the content and message. Often when I interpret dreams for people, I ask them to type up the dream instead of verbalizing it to me. Many of those who are gifted to interpret dreams, including me, feel it's easier to discern the full understanding of a dream when we see it written down.

As we saw in John 14:26, Jesus promises that the Holy Spirit will help bring His words to our remembrance. One way the Holy Spirit accomplishes this task is through dreams. Jesus also promises in this verse that the Holy Spirit "shall teach you all things." We can ask the Holy Spirit to help us understand our dreams, especially when the content is symbolic or abstract. Many individuals have complained that they don't have the gift of dream of interpretation. As believers, however, we all are connected to the Person who has all understanding—the Holy Spirit. Although I feel that God has given me a gift of dream interpretation, there have been times that I have read people's dreams and have been completely at a loss. After asking the Holy Spirit to open my understanding, a supernatural download of insight comes from heaven.

The Middle of the Night

Many times, God has given me profound dreams and revelations that cause me to awaken in the middle of the night. The communication within the dreams is fresh in my mind when I wake up at 2:00 or 3:00 a.m., but too often I will tell myself that I will remember the dreams when I awaken later to start my day. Yet sadly, when I get up at that later time, I've almost totally forgotten what was clear to me hours earlier.

If a dream awakens you in the middle of the night, don't risk missing an important message from God. It may be an inconvenience, but take the time to jot down (even if in shorthand) some notes about your dream. This is another key that will help you recall in the morning your dream activity of the previous night. This is very important if you are an intercessor. Dreams in the night often reveal your prayer assignment for the day ahead.

Once, I was in a foreign nation and the Lord had given me a dream about the leader of the nation. When I awoke, I saw that it was 2:00 a.m. I had just fallen asleep at midnight and was very tired, but God told me to wake up and walk around a photo that I had pulled up on my phone of the nation's leader. I was to walk around it seven times while making decrees from heaven. Amazingly, three days later and a few hours before it was time for me to depart from this nation, I found myself in an in person meeting with the nation's leader! I believe that if I hadn't taken the dream seriously and hadn't taken action, the window for this to happen would never have opened.

Learn the Power of Stillness

Sometimes every self-effort to recall one's dreams seems futile. There have been times that it seemed as if I had dreamed vivid dreams of substance and interest the entire night. Even while asleep I remember thinking, *This is good information. I'm going to remember this when I awake!* However, I would wake up and barely remember bits and pieces of what God had revealed to me in the night. This would cause temporary frustration.

Have you ever misplaced your house or car keys and looked everywhere for them, to no avail? It's not until you sit down and quit looking for the keys that suddenly, as if by inspiration, the memory of where you last placed them pops into your mind. The same holds true when trying to recall your dreams with no success. The overactivity of your conscious mind may be blocking you from recalling a dream. In these instances, I find that the best practice is to go before the Lord and quiet myself. The key here is to learn the power of stillness.

While in a posture of prayer, I ask the Lord to help me re-member my fleeting dream from the previous night. After I ask Him, I quiet my mind and try not to think about remembering the dream. Typically, as I'm softly worshiping the Lord and holding my thoughts still before Him, at some point the dream comes back to me clearly.

Isaiah 30:15 says that "in quietness and confidence shall be your strength." There is a place in the quiet with God where we learn to gain confidence in His ability to strengthen us. This includes strengthening us by bringing back to our remem-brance content from the dream realm that we need to help us fulfill His will in our lives. Also, God may give you further revelation into what you dream as you meditate on what was revealed to you.

What to Remember

There are some key elements you should attempt to remember with each and every dream. Often, individuals become over-whelmed when attempting to interpret or understand a dream, but dissecting your dream into pieces will help you tremen-dously. Learning to look for the following core attributes of your dreams will help your mind process and interpret your dreams more easily.

First, try to remember your emotional state within a dream. A sense of fear or panic can help you discern if a dream is com-ing from a demonic source or some unresolved soul issue. (We will discuss these sources more in-depth in chapters 4 and 5.) A sense of joy, peace, or satisfaction could be a sign that a dream is from God and that He is communicating His desire for you to achieve these emotional states in real life. Also, the emotions surrounding a dream help convey the urgency or seriousness of that dream. Some dreams carry more gravity than others and may require your immediate attention.

Second, try to remember the geography and/or location within a dream. Where a dream takes place has great signifi cance and meaning. The locality can convey much to you about the dream's purpose. I have had several dreams where I'm in a distinct city or nation. God often uses these types of dreams to alert me that He desires for me to go to these places in real life. Also, there is often a specific assignment or task He may have for me at each locality. There have been times that I have dreamed about a city or nation, and within a few days I have been invited to visit that place.

Also, God may use the localities within dreams to place His finger upon parts of our inner being or life that need healing or restoration. I knew a woman who kept dreaming about a house she used to own many years ago. She kept dreaming about being in the house and cleaning out the rooms within. When I questioned her, she revealed that it was a home she had formerly owned with her ex husband. She had suffered betrayal and trauma within that marriage. God was figuratively telling her through the dream that she still needed deep healing from this past relationship.

Third, it is also important to try to remember key characters within your dream. *Who* appears in your dream means a lot. Is the person someone who represents goodness or provokes pleasant feelings for you within your dream? Or does he or she provoke feelings of fear, agitation, or intimidation? The *who* doesn't always have to be a person. It can also be an animal. Many people have experienced unfriendly animals chasing or attacking them in a dream. This is never a good sign. (We'll also talk more about that in chapter 5.)

Fourth, make an effort to try to remember your activity and actions within a dream. What were you doing? What were others doing? Were you being chased? Were you arguing with someone? Were you building something? Were the actions within the dream negative or positive? The activity in a dream gives you a strong indication of the messages being communicated.

Fifth and last, remembering the conversations that take place within a dream is important. This is especially true with God-given dreams. Words have meaning, purpose, and life when they proceed from God. John 6:63 says, "The words that I speak to you are spirit, and they are life." Often, the words within a dream carry more weight and have more meaning than the other elements in the dream. Learn to recollect what you yourself say, what others say to you, and what you may hear elsewhere in a dream. These are important clues to the meaning of the dream.

A Few More Pointers for Dream Recall

So far in this chapter, I have shared five keys to help you better remember your dreams:

—The first key is to develop a mindset of expectation for having dreams.
—The second key is to have the means readily available by your bedside to record your dreams.
—The third key is to make sure not to miss opportunities in the night to immediately recall your dreams when God awakens you.
—The fourth key is learning the power of stillness in quieting yourself before the Lord.
—The fifth and final key is to try to recollect certain key elements or main details from your dreams.

In discussing that fifth key, I also shared five of what I consider to be the most important details to remember within a dream itself: your emotional state, the geography/location, *who* appears, your activity/actions, and any conversations.

These are all important things to keep in mind when recalling your dreams. There are many other elements, however, that can be used to help you remember and interpret a dream. For example, you may recall elements of a dream such as symbols, numbers, and colors, any of which could help you interpret its meaning. Being on the lookout for such elements within a dream causes us to continually sharpen our skills at recalling and interpreting the dreams we do receive.

Another thing you can do to help recall your dreams is to consider the 5 W's. A good rule of thumb is to ask yourself *Who, What, When, Where,* and *Why?* about your dreams. This is a heuristic approach often taught to students to help them with reading comprehension. The 5 W's are also used in information gathering and law-enforcement investigations. In detective work, for example, these 5 W's help determine the details surrounding a crime, the perpetrator of the crime, the motive, and other information that is needed to arrest and prosecute a suspect. Yet I also teach the 5 W's method as a quick and easy way for people to ask themselves questions that will help them remember, discern, and better understand the supernatural dreams they are experiencing.

It May Seem Simple

There are many mysteries within the Bible and the kingdom of God. Many desire to know things like who the "Two Witnesses" are in the book of Revelation, what the chariot of fire was that took up Elijah, or how Enoch was translated to heaven with God. I have always wondered about a simpler mystery in the Bible, however, one of the most powerful and well-known dream encounters—Jacob's ladder dream. My question has always been, *How was Jacob able to dream, let alone sleep, on a bed of rocks?* Look at Genesis 28:10–12:

> Now Jacob went out from Beersheba and went toward Haran.
> So he came to a certain place and stayed there all night, because

the sun had set. And he took one of the stones of that place and put it at his head, and he lay down in that place to sleep. Then he dreamed, and behold, a ladder was set up on the earth, and its top reached to heaven; and there the angels of God were ascending and descending on it.

Scripture tells us that Jacob made a stone his pillow. I believe this makes his account even more supernatural. Jacob was able to both sleep and dream resting his head on a stone. However, I suggest that for most of us, it's better to be comfortable when sleeping. This advice may seem simple and basic, but your comfort level will affect your ability to obtain the proper rest you need, which will increase the chance that you will achieve a dream state.

Also, as I said earlier, the first few moments upon waking are the best time to try to recall your dreams. But waking up with a sharp neck pain or a hurting back will distract your mind. Usually when pain or discomfort is present in the body, it temporarily overrides our other senses. Being able to awake rested and without discomfort will help keep your mind undistracted so that you can better recall your dreams.

Patience Is a Virtue

When you first attempt to recall your dreams and fail, it can be a source of frustration. There have been many days when I knew I had had some profound dream and could only remember glimpses of it. I racked my brain, trying to remember with little to no success. I will explain in chapter 10 (which is about decoding *déjà vu*) why sometimes God actually doesn't allow us to remember all the details of our dreams. Most of the time, however, if you are intentional and strategic about remembering your dreams, you will experience great success.

There is one word we must remember during the dream recollection process. That word is *patience*. "Patience is a virtue" is an ancient proverbial phrase that has survived many cultures and generations. Patience is a virtue because it goes against human instinct for a person to wait on something that he or she strongly desires. Demonstrating patience in recalling your dreams also shows God that you highly value the dreams He may be giving you.

James 1:4 says, "But let patience have its perfect work, that you may be perfect and complete, lacking nothing." This Scripture reveals that it takes some amount of work on our part to exercise patience. Also, this verse reveals that there is always a reward for patience. "That you may be perfect" doesn't mean we will be sinless, faultless, and without blame, like our Lord Jesus Christ. The Greek word here for *perfect* is *teleios*, meaning to be mature or complete.[2] God even uses supernatural dreams to mature and complete us.

As you practice dream recollection, it will become easier and more natural to remember your dreams. Also, you will find yourself becoming more adept at calling to mind details within your dreams, such as locations, atmospheres, colors, numbers, conversations, actions, and emotions. At first, dream remembrance may feel like a cumbersome process, but over time it will become part of an exciting journey of discerning the spiritual atmosphere around you and learning from and about God.

Summary

Remembering your dreams may be challenging, but it is highly possible and doable. As you practice and become intentional about recalling your dreams, you will find yourself developing an increased efficiency in recollecting and understanding them. In this chapter, I have given you some practical keys to help you remember your dreams so that you can be empowered by the supernatural dimension of dreaming.

QUESTIONS FOR REFLECTION

1. Why is it important to actively try to remember your dreams?

2. How does your attitude toward dreams affect your recollection of them? How has what you read in this chapter helped you develop more of a mindset of expectancy about dreaming?

3. What are the 5 W's to ask after having a dream? What are some other dream elements to think about that might help you with dream recall?

4. Why is being comfortable while you sleep important to your dream recollection? What can you do to make your sleep time more comfortable?

two

Activate Your
Dream Life Now

For ages, dreams have been a source of fear for some people and a fascination for others. Those who have had the privilege of receiving supernatural dreams from God are often faced with the question, *How do I receive more dreams from God?* In this chapter, we will discuss some practical insights I have gained from personal experience and from working with others that will help us answer this question and also help you activate your dream life.

God has allowed me to conduct several dream teaching sessions and workshops. One of the most frequent questions people propose to me is, "Why don't I dream more?" Some report having only a few dreams per year, and some say they have had only a few within their lifetime. The topic of prophetic dreams is of great interest to these individuals, but they feel highly frustrated because they feel their own dream lives are inactive.

These individuals are often shocked by the answer I give them: "Simply ask God to speak to you in dreams." That's the first key to having more supernatural dreams. The Bible says in James 4:2, "You do not have because you do not ask." Too often, we limit this Scripture to God meeting only our material needs, but it also applies to our level of communication from Him. Praying a basic prayer of petition, asking God to communicate with you via dreams, pays great spiritual dividends in your life.

Years ago, I approached a co-worker in his office and shared with him, "God gave me a dream for you last night!"

He sat back in his chair, sighed, and grabbed his forehead while exclaiming, "I'm doomed!"

For some reason, he equated a dream from God with a message of judgment. However, I explained to him that God had given me a revelation about a potential career promotion that would soon present itself. He was relieved to know that the message from God was one meant to give him guidance.

This same co-worker shared with me that he had never in his life had a dream. I was amazed. This was my first time meeting someone who had never dreamed. I shared with him that dreams are commonplace and that if he desired for God to speak with him in this way, he should simply ask God! He wasn't a religious man, but he agreed to follow these instructions. A few weeks later, this gentleman came to my desk elated that he had experienced his first dream. He was super elated that God had answered his prayer. What a blessing to receive his first dream after 55-plus years of life.

Being Intentional

Because the things of God are precious and sacred, how we steward them affects whether God increases us in the Spirit. This principle also holds true for the dreams we receive that come from God. Both my wife, Jessica, and I have learned to be good stewards of our dreams.

There are two practical ways that we can be good stewards of our dreams. The first method is by being intentional about remembering our dreams. My wife and I help each other not only to remember our dreams, but to understand what God has been speaking to us in the night hours. When I worked a secular job, every morning I would send my wife an email saying good morning to her. After she responded, my next email would almost always include the same question: "Did you have any dreams last night?"

If I didn't ask the question, sometimes Jessica would beat me to the punch. My wife is a very active dreamer, and I'm always interested to hear how God is not only speaking to her, but also to my family and me, or to the Body of Christ, through the messages God gives her in the night hours.

As Jessica and I learned to be intentional about encouraging one another to share our dreams, we discovered that our minds began to program themselves to actively remember dreams easily in the morning. The number of dreams we struggled to remember has decreased over time, and it has become easier and easier to recollect not only a dream message, but the specific details of a dream. As you become intentional and consistent about recollecting your own dreams, you'll discover that it will become more natural to do so, and you'll do it with greater ease.

God Promises Increase

The second practical way to be a good steward of our dreams deals with the action we take in response to what God reveals to us. When we pray, one of the ways He answers us is through the instructions or revelations within our dreams. I have encountered many individuals who were still seeking God on things that He had already responded to or given answers for through their dreams. At times, God gives instructions in dreams that we must take seriously and obey.

The book of Acts correlates an increase of the measure of the Holy Spirit upon our lives with God communicating to us through dreams and visions. Acts 2:17 says, "And it shall come to pass in the last days, says God, that I will pour out of My Spirit on all flesh; your sons and your daughters shall prophesy, your young men shall see visions, your old men shall dream dreams." We often don't connect the dots between our level of obedience and its effect on our relationship with the Holy Spirit. Scripture reveals this divine connection to us in Acts 5:32, which says He is "the Holy Spirit whom God has given to those who obey Him." God promises to release a greater measure of the Holy Spirit upon those who obey Him. With this new measure of the Holy Spirit comes an increase of revelations through prophecy, visions, and dreams, according to Acts 2:17.

Years ago, I spent an evening praying for deliverance from hardship that I was experiencing. My vehicle had been repossessed, and to make matters worse, my electricity was cut off in my home. I had experienced my automobile being repossessed once before, but never had I encountered this level of financial distress. That night, I had a dream that I was at a local pastor's home, giving him a strong prophetic word of correction about an assignment from God that he had neglected. When I awoke, I was frustrated because I had begged God for wisdom to help me overcome this tough season in my life, and He was speaking to me about something that seemed insignificant at the time.

Later that day, I sat again on my couch and prayed about my financial situation. The Holy Spirit didn't speak to me about money, but reminded me of the dream from the previous night. I figured at this point that it was better to obey God and worry about my circumstances later. I didn't have a vehicle, so I had to humble myself and call my friends Derrick and Tamiko to ask to borrow their Ford Expedition. They drove the vehicle over to my home, and after dropping them off, I proceeded to visit the pastor from the previous night's dream.

After reaching this pastor's home, I shared the prophetic word from the Lord with him. I was surprised at how readily he confirmed and received the message from God. Before I left, however, he looked at me intently and asked, "Demontae, how are your finances?"

I asked, "Why?"

He said, "God spoke to me that you have a heavy financial need in your life."

Heavy was an understatement. I had a whale of a financial burden weighing on me. The pastor went into his office and came out with a check for $3,000 with my name on it. It was the exact amount I needed to catch up on all my delinquent bills.

Had I not obeyed what God had shown me in the dream, I would have missed both an opportunity to speak into this pastor's life, and also a tremendous blessing. I was praying to God about finances, and He answered me through a dream. The answer didn't come in direct form for me, but the instruction about someone else contained the missing link of obedience that would connect me to my own personal breakthrough. When we neglect obeying or partnering with the voice of God in our dreams, there's a chance that we are short-circuiting our own supernatural favor.

Being intentional about remembering our dreams, and taking action to obey any instructions from God within the dreams, makes for good stewardship. When you practice both of these acts, you will become excited about the dreams you receive from God. By stewarding our dreams in these two practical ways, both Jessica and I have noticed that the frequency and depth of our dreams from God have increased. Also, we have discovered that more prophetic dreams are fulfilled in our lives as we properly steward our dreams.

Put the Word to Work

Romans 10:17 says, "So then faith comes by hearing, and hearing by the word of God." What we see, hear, and digest from God's Word can have a direct correlation to our faith. God has blessed me with a healing ministry that did not come by accident, but by careful study of the Scriptures pertaining to divine healing. I discovered that the same principle applies to increasing one's dream life. Studying more of what God's Word says about dreaming can help activate your faith to dream.

In seasons when the frequency of prophetic dreams would decrease in my life, I would open up the Bible and read about several individuals who had vivid dreams from God. Jacob's heavenly dream in Genesis 28, Daniel's revelatory dream in Daniel 7, and Joseph's dreams in Genesis 37 are some of my first go-to Scriptures when I am seeking to enlarge my faith for dreams. Reading these passages helps me remember that God speaks through dreams.

Reading these verses about the Bible's dreamers will help you understand not only how God speaks in dreams, but the different ways that He speaks. You may already be experiencing God speaking to you in similar ways as He did with the saints of old. As you do a careful search of the Word, you will find commonalities in how God spoke to them in olden times and how He may be speaking to you now. Every time I study the dream stories of the Bible, my expectancy for new and exciting dreams in my own life peaks.

A Holy Spirit Promise

The Scriptures also help us realize that dreams and visions are one of the promises for those who have received the infilling of the Holy Spirit. This promise is so powerful that it is found in both the Old and New Testaments. In the Old Testament, Joel 2:28 says, "And it shall come to pass afterward that I will pour out My Spirit on all flesh; your sons and your daughters shall prophesy, your old men shall dream dreams, your young men shall see visions." In the New Testament, the apostle Peter reiterates this prophetic utterance in Acts 2:17.

I asked the Lord why the promise of dreams and visions attached to the outpouring of the Holy Spirit was so important. He spoke to my heart that when believers stop seeing and receiving from Him supernaturally (in dreams and visions), they begin to decrease in faith and lose sight of the hope of God for their lives. Proverbs 29:18 (KJV) declares, "Where there is no vision, the people perish . . ." This doesn't mean that people literally die, but it does mean that part of their focus and expectation from God dies off. Also, they suffer as they lack the counsel of God.

This principle is demonstrated in Genesis with the dreamer Joseph. His interpretation of Pharaoh's dream allowed Egypt to avoid suffering starvation during the seven years of famine. Also, it allowed Egypt to be in a position to service other nations and save the posterity of Israel during the great dearth. A dream and an interpretation of a dream, and acting upon both of those, helped preserve lives and communities.

The key here is to ask for more of the Holy Spirit. If you have not received the baptism of the Holy Spirit, you are missing out on a powerful new dimension of relationship with God (see Acts 2:4; 19:1–6). If you have been baptized with the Holy Spirit but are not experiencing dreams or revelations from God, then you may be in need of a fresh touch from the Holy Spirit. Many of the same apostles and disciples who were baptized with the Spirit in Acts 2 were also praying in Acts 4, where it says that "they were all filled with the Holy Spirit" (verse 31).

Imagine a glass that has water in it but over time has become half full. Many of us need a fresh dose of the Holy Spirit. There have been seasons in my life when God has given me a time of refreshing (see Acts 3:19), and almost immediately in those

39

times there has been a noticeable and measurable increase of dreams, prophetic words, and visions in my life. Increased revelations, especially in dreams, are one by-product of pursuing a greater infilling and intimacy with the Holy Spirit.

Times and Seasons Matter

One day, God told me to go back and read all the prophetic words, dreams, and visions recorded in my prophetic journals. As I read through years of archives, I noticed that two certain months of the year consistently had three times the amount of journal entries in contrast to the other months. It was then that I realized these months held a special importance in my spiritual life.

As I began to research these two months, I realized that both coincided with certain Hebraic holidays and festivals. Ancient religious leaders and early Church fathers considered these special times of the year to be of great religious, historical, and spiritual significance. Also, I once heard the legendary seer prophet Bob Jones say that the Lord would visit him every September in a dream or a vision with a special message for the Body of Christ. I knew I was on to something.

During an online dream teaching, I polled those in attendance about how many had noticed that during a certain month of the year, certain spiritual activities—especially supernatural dreams—would increase in their lives. After pondering it for a time, several professed that indeed God dealt with them more heavily during a certain month of the year. Often, the month of increased spiritual activity and dreams for many people is the time frame surrounding their birthday.

Why does God choose to operate this way? A study of the Bible reveals that God operates through times, seasons, and cycles. In the book of Genesis, we see God's divine intentionality during His creative process for Earth and humankind. The

Bible says in Ecclesiastes 3:1, "To everything there is season, a time for every purpose under heaven." Discerning the times of God helps us more easily tap into the special graces, wisdom, and favor of God that may be available to us in different seasons of our lives.

I have learned to activate the supernatural dimension of dreams and revelations within my life through discerning prophetic seasons and cycles. You can do the same. First, determine in which month or season of your life there may exist a special window of grace from God. Once you discern this through intentional observation, it's very important to increase the time you spend in that month or season in the Word, prayer, worship, and focusing your mind on the things of God. Increasing your pursuit of God during that season will cause you to take full advantage of the spiritual window open to you. Try this, and you will most likely notice a measurable increase in the frequency, depth of content, and impact of your dreams.

Activating Your Dream Life

I want to conclude this chapter with an easy-to-do exercise to help you activate your dream life. This exercise has a couple of prerequisites: avoid watching any television or engaging in social media activity for a few hours before bedtime, and make sure to have a pen and paper beside your bed (or somewhere nearby) that you can easily access upon waking up. A digital recorder or voice recorder on your smartphone is acceptable as well. Then follow these steps:

1. Spend at least thirty minutes reading the Bible before bed.
2. After reading the Bible, engage in a time of worship and prayer. It's very important near the end of your time of prayer that you ask God to speak to you as you rest.

3. Be specific about what area of life you desire God to communicate with you about (for example, your relationships, your finances, your ministry, your health, etc.).

4. When you awaken in the morning, grab your notepad or voice recorder and attempt to journal your dream (if any) from the previous night.

5. If you have difficulty recollecting what you dreamed about, spend a few minutes praying and asking the Holy Spirit to bring back to your memory any details or dream information.

6. Later in the day, revisit what you wrote down or recorded in an audio file. Often, throughout the day, more glimpses or details of your dream will surface into your conscious mind.

7. During the day, pray over your dream. If you are unsure of the dream's meaning, ask God for more insight. He may choose to answer you in that moment, or He may give you another dream that brings more insight into the first one, so be ready!

Have fun doing this exercise meant to activate your dream life. Relax and don't stress. "Let patience have its perfect work," as James 1:4 says. Don't become frustrated if you don't receive a heavenly message the first night. Exercise faith and patience by following the steps in this exercise again each night, or select one night of each week that you will try it.

Summary

In this chapter, we have discussed things that we can do as believers, both naturally and supernaturally, to help enhance our dream life. Many of these things are practical in nature, but they help unlock new realms of God communicating with us as we rest. Being intentional about remembering our dreams, and being good stewards over our dreams, are essential elements in deepening our dream encounters. Partnering with the Holy Spirit becomes a very rewarding and exciting journey when we learn to activate our dream life.

<hr/>

QUESTIONS FOR REFLECTION

1. What is the simple but often overlooked "ask" that you can do to increase your dream life?

2. We talked about being good stewards of our dream life by intentionally practicing dream recall and by actively responding to our God given dreams. What can you do to become better at this kind of stewardship?

3. How does the infilling of the Holy Spirit relate to activating your dream life?

4. What things do you notice in your own life that cause you to dream more?

three

What Happens When We Sleep

There are routine and simple things in life that we often take for granted. These life functions, processes, and natural occurrences are often considered mundane, yet they are essential to our very existence. Sleep is one of these natural functions of humankind and many other organisms.

Sleep may seem like a routine process, yet it is indispensable to our well-being, vitality, and much more. I believe that understanding what happens when we sleep is important to understanding how God uses this essential life function not only for our maintenance, but also to release supernatural dreams to us.

Sleep in the Bible

The Scriptures intimate to us how God can powerfully use our time of rest to communicate with us and perform miracles. The book of Genesis gives a powerful account of how before

God created Eve, He put Adam into a deep sleep and created her from Adam's rib:

> And the LORD God caused a deep sleep to fall on Adam, and he slept; and He took one of his ribs, and closed up the flesh in its place. Then the rib which the LORD God had taken from man He made into a woman, and He brought her to the man.
>
> Genesis 2:21–22

Imagine Adam falling asleep and then awakening to find another human—the first other human he had ever seen—standing before him. What an amazing experience this must have been for Adam!

I believe that both the sleep and dream processes speak to the creative nature of God. God demonstrated His Creator dimension in Genesis when He created (or some say re-created) the Earth, living organisms, the firmament, and humankind. The book of John opens up in chapter 1 by explicitly describing the Lord Jesus Christ as a Master Creator:

> In the beginning was the Word, and the Word was with God, and the Word was God. He was in the beginning with God. All things were made through Him, and without Him nothing was made that was made.
>
> John 1:1–3

Creative physiological processes take place when we sleep. If you experience dreams from God, you soon learn how He creatively uses imagery, scenery, and symbolism to communicate His mind to you.

There are many accounts in the Bible of God using sleep to guide, help, and communicate with people. There are some very popular accounts in the Old Testament, such as Joseph interpreting Pharaoh's dreams to help prepare the nation of

Egypt for famine (see Genesis 41:14–36). The New Testament opens with another Joseph being guided by God in dreams in an effort to protect his family (see Matthew 2:13–23). God does everything with divine intention. I believe that sleep in both of these men's lives reveals to us the power of God not only to speak to us in the night, but even to use sleep to bring the miraculous into our lives.

Purposes of Sleep

There are two things most humans commonly enjoy and need: food and sleep. A good night of rest, or even a daytime nap, refreshes and reenergizes our body and mind. Although we all sleep every night, rarely do we take time to think about the power and purpose sleep serves. Adult humans spend nearly one-third of their lives sleeping. This fact alone reveals the tremendous importance sleep plays in our daily lives.

A consistent lack of sleep is called *sleep deprivation* and can lead to an individual experiencing a physical, mental, and emotional breakdown. Some of the side effects of sleep deprivation are mental fog or confusion, mood swings, high blood pressure, a weakened immune system, irritability, lack of motivation, and visual impairment. *Medical News Today* reports this:

> Not only does insufficient sleep impair attention and judgment, but prolonged sleep deprivation raises the risk of type 2 diabetes, high blood pressure, obesity, and respiratory disease.
>
> More recently, some have found that sleeplessness increases the risk of kidney disease and premature death.[1]

Although this list is not exhaustive of the many symptoms that may result from sleep deprivation, it goes to show the importance of getting proper rest and sleep.

In contrast, there are many benefits of proper rest, which experts suggest is seven to eight hours of sleep per night. Some of the benefits to our mind are increased mental focus, a more positive mood, and increased memory retention. Some of the benefits to our body are better weight management, improved metabolism, repair of muscle tissue, and a healthier immune system.

We often consider things such as a new job, a new vehicle, finances, or opportunities as blessings from God, but rarely do we consider proper rest as a gift from Him. Yet Scripture reveals to us that a good night's rest is a blessing from God. Psalm 127:2 says, "For so He gives His beloved sleep." Let's examine the natural phenomenon of sleep and its physiological characteristics, along with what happens during each sleep stage and how God uses each of those stages.

The Four Stages of Sleep

After careful research and study, scientists have discovered that there are different cycles of sleep. They have aptly named what takes place during each of these sleep cycles the four stages of sleep. The first three stages, involving non-rapid eye movement (or NREM) sleep, are named NREM-1, NREM-2, and NREM-3. The fourth stage is known as REM sleep, based on the rapid eye movement that happens during this final stage.

Advanced medical and scientific equipment allows researchers to measure the characteristics of these sleep stages, provide measurable information, and diagnose sleep disorders. Several tests can be used during a sleep study to gain insight into a person's sleep cycles, including an EMG (electromyography) test that measures muscle movement, an EEG (electroencephalography) test that measures brain wave activity, an EOG (electrooculogram) that measures eye movement, and an ECG (electrocardiogram) that measures heart rate activity. Let's look at what some of these tests and other scientific studies have helped us discover about each sleep stage.

Stage One

In layman's terms, we call this NREM-1 stage "falling asleep." In this sleep stage your eyes are closed, but you haven't yet entered into a deep rest. It is still easy for a person in stage one to be awakened, especially by external stimuli.

This first stage of sleep may last up to ten minutes. Breathing and heart rate remain regular. People awakened from this stage of sleep may not even realize that they were asleep.

A person's eyes often become heavy and will close during this stage. However, only non-rapid eye movement occurs during this sleep stage, which is often called "light sleep."

Stage Two

As a person enters this NREM-2 stage of rest, the body's temperature decreases and the heart rate begins to slow down. Also, a person's muscles are completely relaxed by stage two. This phase of sleep often lasts up to 25 minutes. An individual can still be easily awakened, but not as easily as in stage one of the sleep cycle.

The brain begins to do something interesting in this stage of sleep, creating what are called "sleep spindles." These sleep spindles are generated by the thalamus, which is an egg-shaped gland in the center of our brain. One of the most important functions of the thalamus is to monitor, regulate, and relay sensory and motor information between the body and the brain. Four of our five senses are regulated in this way by the thalamus—touch, taste, hearing, and vision. Sleep spindles are bursts of neural sigma waves from the thalamus to the body. These waves help relay information back to the brain concerning what specific nerves control what specific muscles. Also, this process helps with memory retention and compartmentalization.

A person experiencing sleep deprivation would miss this phase of rest and experience memory loss, mental fatigue, and a decrease of muscular coordination. I can think of two world champion boxers who broke from their regular training routine, instead spending their nights partying, drinking, and not sleeping properly. Then during their bouts they were easily beaten, although they were renowned champions. Much of this had to do with their loss of the brain-muscle coordination that proper sleep brings. The sleep spindles, or bundles of sigma wave signals, during stage two of sleep help us function at our maximum potential in regard to cognition and movement.

Stage Three

Stage three is considered the beginning of the deep sleep phase of the sleep cycle. At this NREM-3 stage, your brain emits delta or slow waves that further relax the body and mind in order to facilitate healthy tasks, such as muscle repair and the restoration of the immune system. As the body becomes fully relaxed, the sleeper's heart rate and breathing slow down significantly. During this phase, the body goes into self-repair mode and begins to reenergize itself. Muscle tissue repairs and cell regeneration happen in stage three. Ultraviolet light from the sun, along with physical stressors, biochemical stressors, and free radicals in our body, all cause damage to the DNA in our cells. The need to be repaired during rest from any damage is especially true for our neurons, which are the body's signal senders and receptors. They are active nonstop all day, but can be repaired while the body is in the deep sleep state.

I believe that God created phenomena in nature and within the human experience that mirror the Gospel message. I think this third stage of sleep is one of those mirrors. Think about this: It's interesting to find that after enduring physical torture and suffering, Jesus arose on the *third* day. The Nicene Creed, a well-known statement of faith, declares that Jesus "suffered death and was buried, and rose again on the third day." The body's rejuvenating function in the third phase of sleep serves as a microcosm of God's greater power of resurrection demonstrated at the cross with the Lord Jesus Christ. Also, we find that the number 3 is related to healing, regeneration, and restoration in the Old Testament: "Come, and let us return to the LORD; for He has torn, but He will heal us; He has stricken, but He will bind us up. After two days He will revive us; on the third day He will raise us up . . ." (Hosea 6:1–2).

A person awakened from the third stage of sleep will often feel slightly groggy or disoriented for a few moments before becoming fully alert. A lack of deep third-stage sleep can lead to catabolism, which is the breakdown of the muscles and the body's cells. This stage of sleep lasts on average thirty minutes and is very necessary for our health and mental alertness so we can accomplish our daily tasks well.

Stage Four

Stage four of the sleep process is where things get interesting! This stage of sleep is called the rapid eye movement stage, or simply REM sleep. Can you guess what differentiates this stage from the previous three? Yes, you guessed right—the sleeper's eyes move rapidly. You may have witnessed other people sleeping and noticed that their eyes flutter for several minutes at a time. What you are witnessing is someone in REM sleep.

The REM stage of sleep is where most of our dreams occur. It is also the state where the most vivid and intense dreams occur. At this phase, the sleeper's heart rate and breathing increase versus decrease. Also, brain waves and mental activity become measurably more active and heightened. The brain's activity in stage four of sleep most closely resembles the regular brain activity we would see in an individual who is awake.

The REM sleep stage has two phases: tonic and phasic REM sleep. During phasic REM sleep, the eyes move rapidly for minutes at a time. Also, there exists a greater degree of brain activity and an increased potential for dreaming. However, the

51

physical body of the sleeper experiences just the opposite—
a lessened degree of physical motor activity, less response to
external stimuli, and less environmental alertness. During the
tonic phase of REM sleep, the eyes do not move as much, the
potential for dreaming decreases, and the physical body is more
susceptible to being aroused or affected by environmental and
external stimuli.

Stage four REM sleep often lasts ten minutes during the first
cycle of sleep, but increases in length with each progressive
sleep cycle. The REM stage in the final cycle before a person
awakens can last up to an hour. This is one of the reasons many
people report dreaming longer and in more detail during the
early morning hours. In fact, I have noticed that many of my
dreams happen around 5:00 a.m., after I have been sleeping for
several hours and have gone through a number of sleep cycles.

I discovered the fascinating fact that God has put in place a
protective mechanism for us during this fourth stage of sleep.
In REM sleep, while the mind becomes more active, the body
becomes very static and nearly immobilized. I believe that God
set this in place as a safety measure so that people don't harm
themselves during REM sleep, while they are dreaming. The
mind often has difficulty during the sleep process discerning
between a dream and reality, which could cause a person to try
to act out his or her dream. Have you heard of people fighting or arguing with someone in their sleep? This especially
happens for those of us engaged in spiritual warfare. God put
a physiological check in place during this REM sleep phase,
however, to protect us and those who may be lying in the bed
with us. Amazing!

God's Super on the Natural

There's a saying that the supernatural is just God's super placed
on top of our natural. Although sleep is a natural process, God

has the ability to make it a supernatural experience. This was certainly the case for the patriarch Abraham. After Abraham returned from victory in battle, he encountered the high priest of Salem, Melchizedek, and tithed to him. Genesis 15:1 tells us, "After these things the word of the LORD came to Abram in a vision, saying, 'Do not be afraid, Abram. I am your shield, your exceedingly great reward.'"

God began to speak to Abraham, reassuring him of His favor, protection, and blessing upon his life. Also, God promised Abraham the one thing that he lacked and longed for greatly—a male heir. In addition, He promised to give him a great deal of land as his possession. Abraham was then instructed as part of the covenant being established between God and himself to sacrifice certain animals. He cut them in two and arranged the pieces opposite each other, as was the custom in making covenants at the time, and then Genesis 15:12 (NIV) tells us, "As the sun was setting, Abram fell into a deep sleep, and a thick and dreadful darkness came over him."

God purposely placed Abram into what the Bible calls "a deep sleep." Why was this done? I believe that God wanted to suspend many of Abraham's natural senses because what He desired to communicate to him was so important that God could leave no room for misinterpretation or miscommunication. It seems that God spoke to Abraham audibly and clearly while he was deep within the dream state.

Also, while Abraham was asleep, another powerful thing happened that sealed his covenant with God: "When the sun had set and darkness had fallen, a smoking firepot with a blazing torch appeared and passed between the pieces. On that day the LORD made a covenant with Abram . . ." (Genesis 15:17–18 NIV). I believe that the Lord caused Abraham to be asleep while all of this was happening as a sign that it was God who was initiating and taking ultimate responsibility for fulfilling the supernatural covenant made that day!

Summary

God has provided sleep as a natural mechanism for our body to heal, our memories to be properly stored within our brain, our cells to be repaired, our immune system to be built up, and much more. In addition to sleep serving so many functions for our physical bodies, God has provisioned the REM stage of our sleep to serve as a powerful mechanism through which He can speak to us in dreams during our times of rest. Although not every dream comes from God (which we will discuss in the next couple of chapters), many dreams do come from Him, and these should not be overlooked.

QUESTIONS FOR REFLECTION

1. How is God's creative nature revealed in the sleep and dream processes?
2. What are a few of the reasons that proper sleep is a blessing from God? What blessings do you notice in your life when you get the proper rest?
3. What are some of the negatives that result from a lack of sleep, or sleep deprivation? What steps are you taking to make sure you get adequate sleep so you can avoid these things and enjoy the built-in benefits of proper rest?
4. What stage of sleep do most dreams occur in? I mentioned that I tend to dream the most around 5:00 a.m., when this stage lasts its longest. Have you noticed any similar patterns in your dream life? (If not, be on the lookout for them.)

four

Dream but Discern

There are supernatural dreams that emanate from the spirit realm. Not all dreams, however, are from a supernatural source. Some dreams are from a more natural source. It is important to be understanding and discern these dreams, and separate them from dreams that come directly from God.

Dreams that don't emanate from any spiritual source still may potentially reveal information to us that can help us during our life journey. These dreams I term "soulish dreams." They are dreams produced by our own mind. Soulish dreams are the most common type of dreams that most people experience. In this chapter, I will discuss some of the sources and purposes of these soulish dreams.

Don't Be a Busybody

Our brains can be compared to organic supercomputers that daily perform a plethora of simultaneous tasks. When we awaken, our mind has to coordinate our skeletal-muscular activity to allow us to arise from bed. It must prioritize our day, remember things of importance from yesterday, and then help us accomplish every activity throughout the day. Every activity involves the brain in some way. Even while we are asleep, the brain still is at work.

Every computer system works with inputs and outputs, meaning some type of data or code is inputted and the computer hashes out results. An example would be the way the physical movement of a computer mouse results in the cursor moving on the computer screen. Our brain functions in a similar fashion: throughout the day, it is receiving inputs that it must process and sort out. If we are engaged in too many activities and too many conversations within a day, this can often filter over into our time of rest and into our dreams. The Bible reveals this fact in Ecclesiastes 5:3 (KJV): "For a dream cometh through the multitude of business." Or as another translation, the New King James Version, says, "For a dream comes through much activity."

That's right—being a busybody can affect the source and purity of your dreams. Years ago, I noticed that the quality of my dreams diminished when I spent more time talking on the phone with individuals throughout the day and watching TV. It often becomes more difficult for the dreams that God downloads into our spirit to break through into our conscious mind if it is clogged up with too much input from conflicting sources. This is why we must be careful not only about what we hear and see of certain things, but also *how much* we hear and see. While it is okay to watch TV, watching too much may be counterproductive to our spiritual life.

As a minister of the Gospel and a spiritual coach, many times I entertain numerous calls throughout the day from individuals who primarily want to share problems in their life and seek help. Often, their life issues involve high-stress situations, such as relationship problems, health challenges, moral failures, or ministry turmoil. In the past, some of the subject matter from these phone calls would assimilate into my dreams at night, with an accompanying feeling of tension. The Lord taught me that if I would read the Word and pray at the end of each day, even if only for fifteen minutes, that would allow Him time to decompress my mind and purify my soul from the daytime inputs I had received that could continue as stressors in my own life.

Our dream life can be purified and can become more prophetic when we are not being busybodies in matters that don't concern us. A dear friend of mine, Dr. Kim Black, prophesied the word of the Lord to me, saying, "God says your *no* is anointed too!" I knew she meant that God didn't want me to accept every speaking engagement, phone call, request for counseling, or conversation, but to be discerning about my boundaries and times. Being led by the Holy Spirit in our daily life about what has access to our eye and ear gates (and ultimately our heart) will minimize dreams that come "through the multitude of business" and "through much activity." These types of dreams hold the least value and benefit to us.

Your Belly Speaks

Many people believe that the foods they eat can influence dreaming. A common response to someone having a bad dream is, "Did you eat a lot of pizza late at night? It's a pizza dream!" How could food affect our dream life? Yet many have reported experiencing a night of strange, vivid dreams after a late-night pizza-eating binge. Foods contain biochemicals, nutrients, and ingredients that interact with our bodies in a myriad of fashions.

Hormones are generated and released by the glands within our body's endocrine system and serve as our body's chemical messengers. Certain biochemicals in food can cause an increase or decrease of certain hormones in our body. Sugar is one of the chemicals that has the most effect on the body and on our hormones. So the foods we eat affect the chemical messages sent to our brain, which at times may affect our dream state.

Serotonin and melatonin are two naturally occurring hormones in the body that are involved in wakefulness and sleep. High serotonin levels decrease the time of rapid eye movement or REM sleep. Some foods increase our serotonin level. Melatonin is called "the sleep hormone" because one of its functions is to help regulate our body's internal clock and relaxation, which helps promote healthy sleep. Eating foods that are high in melatonin, such as eggs, cherries, nuts, or fish, may help increase the deeper levels of sleep that allow for REM stages of dreaming.

Just as a person's body temperature decreases as he or she progresses through each stage of sleep, causing an individual to feel colder, consuming spicy foods causes your body's internal temperature to rise. Spicy foods eaten late at night may therefore be counterproductive to achieving deep rest. For many years, people have associated bad dreams with eating spicy foods late at night.

My dad called me one day and complained about his previous night's sleep. He had attended an event at a social club the previous evening where he had eaten a dish containing noodles and mushrooms. The mushrooms had an unusual taste, and something inside of him told him to stop eating the dish, but since he was hungry and no other food was available, he finished it. That night, he experienced the most unusual and unpleasant dreams. He described them as taking place in a world that was a mixture of *The Twilight Zone* and *Star Trek*. It seems there may have been some wild mushrooms mixed in with the more common portobello mushrooms. These wild additions produced a psychoactive effect on his mind, which produced strange and unusual dreams.

While certain mushrooms are known to be hallucinogenic, other foods and spices can also have similar effects on individuals, including but not limited to nutmeg, capsaicin in chili peppers, poppy seeds, mulberries, and certain cheeses. Most people who consume these in moderate amounts may experience no changes in their mental state or dreams, but other people may find that their dreams are noticeably affected.

Fasting

Fasting is a vital spiritual practice done not only by Christians, but even by those who adhere to other religious disciplines. A fast involves reducing or eliminating one's food intake for a specified time. One common saying states, "Fasting doesn't change God; it changes you!" This may be true in a spiritual sense, but there are also biochemical changes that take place when we fast that position us to receive more easily from God.

Individuals may partake of different types of fasts. The Daniel fast involves eating only fruits and vegetables, with water as the only liquid. A dry fast involves consuming no food or liquids for a specified number of hours or days. Other modified fasts serve other purposes, but all fasting has some health benefits and likewise spiritual benefits.

I believe one of the hidden benefits of fasting is the impact on our dream life. Reducing our intake of certain foods and liquids (especially sugary ones) allows our body to purge itself of digested ingredients that could negatively impact our sleep and dream state. This same principle applies to us being "clear" to hear God in prayer. Most people who practice fasting in conjunction with sincere prayer report increased dreams, visions, and spiritual sensitivity.

Your Heart Speaks

When decoded, dreams that come from our soul can reveal to us the condition of our "inner man." One of the neurophysiological activities that takes place during our time of rest is our brain processing, categorizing, and compartmentalizing memories. Each of us has internal memory banks that include sensory memory, short-term memory, and long-term memory. Emotionalized memories—those that have a high emotional value attached to them, such as anxiety, trauma, depression, or excitement—are processed during the REM stage of sleep.

We talked in the previous chapter about the egg-shaped gland called the thalamus in the middle of our brain. The thalamus transfers information from our five senses to our cerebral cortex within the brain. One online article explaining the basics of sleep says this about the thalamus: "During most stages of sleep, the thalamus becomes quiet, letting you tune out the external world. But during REM sleep, the thalamus is active, sending the cortex images, sounds, and other sensations that fill our dreams."[1] An unhealthy or damaged thalamus gland can therefore lead to sleep disorders.

REM sleep is the time when memories are processed and when dreams happen. As our memories are being processed, they often filter over into our dream content. This is one reason that many dreams are the products of our subconscious mind and often contain clues to the condition of our soul. Also, such dreams may contain indicators of unresolved issues in our subconscious.

We are all spirits who have a soul and live in a physical body. Our soul is where our mind, will, and emotions abide. Our mind deals with thinking and cognition. The conscious part of our mind deals with thoughts and actions more under our control and awareness. The subconscious mind is less under our control and awareness but retains memory and data that automatically control our responses, behavior, and thinking. Have you ever heard someone say things like, "I don't know why I do what I do," or "I've been this way since I was a little child"? These individuals are unaware that their behavior is being influenced by their subconscious.

The Bible encourages us in Romans 12:2, "And do not be conformed to this world, but be transformed by the renewing of your mind." One of the great transformational benefits of reading and believing the Word of God is that it helps remove negative emotions, negative self-imagery, and negative behaviors from one's subconscious. What modern psychologists call the subconscious, the Bible calls "the heart." A search and study of the word *heart* within the Bible will reveal that Scripture's references to the heart often are not talking about the physical organ of the heart in our body, but rather the "heart" of our mind, which is the subconscious.

We discussed earlier how our brain functions much like an organic computer, which produces outputs based on the inputs it receives. The Bible shares with us a powerful truth related to this in Proverbs 4:23: "Keep your heart with all diligence, for out of it spring the issues of life." The New International Version reads, "Above all else, guard your heart, for everything you do flows from it." In layman's terms, replacing the word *heart* with *mind* or *subconscious* in this verse gives us a deeper understanding of this biblical principle.

Dreams with recurring themes, scenery, or messages often are the by-product of unresolved soul trauma. Trauma is a defensive mechanism of our body in response to overwhelmingly negative events, such as domestic abuse, molestation, witnessing violence, the sudden death of a loved one, or divorce. Because our core personality is formed during childhood, trauma that happens during this period often has the most impact on shaping our worldview, values, behaviors, reactions to situations, and such. Traumatic events that happen in childhood are embedded within our memory. If left unresolved, they not only may affect our behavior and emotions, but also will reveal themselves through our dreams.

One old saying suggests that "time is the healer of all wounds." I strongly disagree with this adage. After many years of counseling and ministering to individuals, I have found this statement to be absolutely false. I have encountered many men and women who were still traumatized by events that took place forty or more years earlier in their lives.

One man in his sixties shared with me how he was having repeated dreams of a little boy opening the front door of his home, as if waiting for someone. When the person the little boy was waiting for didn't appear, the little boy would weep and fall to his knees. The Holy Spirit had me share with the man that he was that little boy in the dream, and that the absence of his father had created a deep feeling of rejection and abandonment in his life that only God could heal.

Although this gentleman was well into adulthood, the unresolved trauma of disappointment, abandonment, and rejection from the absence of his father was still present within his soul. The dreams were indicators that deep healing still needed to take place in his life. His negative memories of trauma that were unprocessed by his brain were responsible for his recurring dreams.

Many of us have experienced dreams like this that weren't necessarily God-given prophetic dreams, but that still held value. God does everything by divine design and purpose. He strategically created the dream mechanism to have a correlation with our memory processing. A careful inquiry of even our soulish dreams will often reveal to us areas of our life that we need to submit to God in prayer, seeking the Holy Spirit for healing, deliverance, or guidance.

Tearing Down Strongholds

The well-known passage 2 Corinthians 10:3–6 concerning "strongholds" is often applied to spiritual warfare teachings:

> For though we walk in the flesh, we do not war according to the flesh. For the weapons of our warfare are not carnal but mighty

in God for pulling down strongholds, casting down arguments
and every high thing that exalts itself against the knowledge of
God, bringing every thought into captivity to the obedience of
Christ, and being ready to punish all disobedience when your
obedience is fulfilled.

This passage may be applicable to battling demonic powers and
foes, but it also has a more widespread application. One of the
greatest spiritual battles that exists is the battle for truth. It is
no coincidence that the Holy Spirit is also called "the Spirit of
truth" (John 14:17) and that Jesus said of Satan "for he is a liar
and the father of it" (John 8:44).

Satan is always working to sell humankind lies, falsehoods,
and deceptions that pervert people's minds from the truth of
God's Word and Spirit. There exists another level of warfare
over the battle for truth that happens at a more personal level.
Often, our own past experiences, prejudices, indoctrinations,
predispositions, or strong desires can skew our view of the
truth. We can make "truths" out of things that are contradic-
tory to reality and God's truth.

During a presidential election year, a prophetic friend of mine
was adamant that a certain candidate would win. He shared
with me multiple dreams that he interpreted as being in support
of his "revelation." I never voiced my opinion or insights on the
matter, but I felt that God had revealed to me that the opposing
candidate would win. My friend was a personal supporter of the
candidate who he felt would win, a vocal advocate of that candidate's party, and very critical of the opposition. Yet when the
election results came in, his candidate lost decisively. My friend
had genuinely believed that he had "heard from God," but he
was mistaken. God showed me that this friend's own strong
prejudices and personal desires had influenced his dream life.

I have seen this phenomenon, which I call *dream contamina-
tion*, bring confusion to several men and women I know. Due to

dream(s) they experienced, these individuals were believing that a certain person was called by God to be their spouse. When no relationship or nuptials happened with the intended object of their affection, they were often left bewildered.

Sometimes the strongholds we have to pull down are not satanic in nature, but rather are vain or inaccurate "imaginations" that don't align with biblical truths. As 2 Corinthians 10:4–5 (KJV) states, the weapons of our spiritual warfare are mighty to the pulling down of strongholds, including "casting down imaginations" and everything else that exalts itself against the knowledge of God. The *Merriam-Webster* defines an *imagination* as a "fanciful or empty assumption."[2] Imaginations can be erroneous belief systems that contradict the Word and will of God. As we grow closer to God, open our heart to His truth, and lay down our own assumptions at His feet, we begin to pick up more of the "mind of Christ" (1 Corinthians 2:16). As the mind of Christ increases within us, our dreams become more prophetic in nature, and our dream life is less contaminated by our own inner strongholds.

Summary

In this chapter, I have discussed how our own soul and subconscious can be the source of certain dreams. But we can lessen the frequency of "soulish dreams" by monitoring our eye and ear gates, especially in regard to our intake of TV shows, social media, and phone conversations about problems and issues. Also, limiting certain foods and spices within our diet lends to minimizing these dreams. Soulish dreams are unprophetic in nature, although in the case of unresolved trauma they may hold some value in helping us identify areas of our life where we may need inner healing. Our desire, however, is to have prophetic or "God dreams" that empower us to fulfill the will of God for our lives and to be blessed in life as we do.

QUESTIONS FOR REFLECTION

1. How can food affect our dreaming? How has food you
   have eaten seemed to affect your dreams? Try to pay attention to how certain foods may cause your dream life
   to fluctuate.

2. What does the Bible say about the business and activity
   of life in connection to dreaming? What changes have
   you noticed in your dream life when you are particu-
   larly busy?

3. What is one way that fasting impacts our dream life?
   Next time you fast, pay attention to whether it affects
   your dreams.

4. What may be the cause of a recurring soulish dream? In
   what way can such dreams hold value and help us move
   forward in life?

five

Those Bad Dreams

There are two types of dreams that are spiritual in nature: those that emanate from the kingdom of darkness and those that come from God. *Demonic dream* is a term used to describe the dreams that originate from the kingdom of darkness. Unwittingly, many people have simply called these "bad dreams" and have neglected their significance. In this chapter, we will discuss what these types of dreams are and what they mean. We will look closely at their purpose, how to discern them when they happen, and even how we can use them against the enemy.

As I mentioned in the previous chapter, God created humans as spirits who have a soul and live in a body. We are three-part beings made in the image and likeness of God—God the Father, the Son, and the Holy Spirit—the three-in-one being of the Trinity (see Genesis 1:26; Mark 12:29; John 17:21). Our spirit is the part of our being that allows us to make contact with and receive messages from the spirit world (whether from the Kingdom of God or the kingdom of darkness). The spirit world is the realm where spiritual activity happens that is imperceptible to our human physical senses. While we are asleep, our conscious mind is more at rest, which allows our spirit to pick up on some of the constant nonstop spiritual activity that is happening in the world around us.

Some of that activity comes from the enemy. The Lord Jesus compares Satan to a thief and says of him in John 10:10, "The thief does not come except to steal, and to kill, and to destroy." What are some of the things that the enemy tries to steal from us? Good health, peace of mind, joy, healthy relationships, salvation, faith, and hope are just a few. The enemy cannot freely do this, so he uses various tactics to accomplish this evil end goal. One tactic he employs to try to steal our peace is demonic dreams.

Bad Dreams as Bad Seeds

Although Satan uses different means to accomplish spiritual thievery, many of his tactics have not changed. In the Garden of Eden, Satan used the cunning art of deception and the power of suggestion to beguile Eve. The power of suggestion is still the *modus operandi* Satan and his minions use. Have you heard of individuals who report things like, "I was driving and something told me to run my car off the bridge and kill myself"? Or individuals who killed their own children and then reported that "something came over me" or "a voice told me to do it"? Those individuals who are not spiritually fortified and who lack a relationship with God are more susceptible to Satan's power of suggestion.

One of the times that the enemy will try to implement thoughts or suggestions into our lives is during our sleep. Satan knows we are slightly more vulnerable to the power of suggestion when we are at rest, because our conscious mind is less active. He will often visit us with dreams that contain messages of failure or fear while we are asleep. If these dreams go unchecked, and if our spirit is not fortified with the Word of God, these dreams have the potential to cause havoc in our lives.

We discover this truth within one of the parables Jesus related in Matthew 13:24–25: "The kingdom of heaven is like a man who sowed good seed in his field; but while men slept, his enemy came and sowed tares among the wheat and went his way." One of the beautiful riches of Jesus' parables is that they often have multiple applications. This parable can be applied to the reaping of the harvest of souls, but it is also *apropos* to our discourse on how Satan attempts to work against us in the dream realm. The man sowing good seed (dreams) in his field is God. The enemy who came and sowed tares (bad dreams) is Satan, the devil.

Note that the sowing of the tares happened "while men slept," at a time when the enemy feels humankind is most vulnerable—during sleep. While we are asleep, the enemy attempts to sneakily deposit these "tares" into our subconscious. The adverse effects of the negative content the enemy deposits often don't manifest in our lives until days, weeks, or months later. Matthew 13:26–27 goes on: "But when the grain had sprouted and produced a crop, then the tares also appeared. So the servants of the owner came and said to him, 'Sir, did you not sow good seed in your field? How then does it have tares?'" Sometimes sickness, misfortune, poverty, an accident, or some other negative incident manifests in our lives for no apparent reason. Most of us fail to correlate the lies the enemy tries to convince us of in our dreams to such incidents.

I am not suggesting, of course, that the enemy's attempts in the night to steal, kill, and destroy will always succeed in having adverse effects on us. The power of suggestion only takes root and has ill effect if the power of our agreement works alongside it. In the Garden of Eden, Satan's power of suggestion only bore fruit when Eve came into agreement with his words through her act of disobedience. Amos 3:3 asks, "Can two walk together, unless they are agreed?" The enemy cannot move further or walk into our lives unless there is some open door or form of agreement on our part.

Often, we are unaware that we have acquiesced to the lies of the enemy, because this activity happens frequently at the subconscious level. That's why it is important to become full of the Word of God by reading and meditating on Scripture as part of our lifestyle. Digesting the Bible in increased measures causes our inner spirit and faith to become stronger. Ephesians 6:16 admonishes us about the importance of "above all, taking the shield of faith with which you will be able to quench all the fiery darts of the wicked one." One type of fiery dart the enemy attempts to launch against us is negative thoughts. This verse in Ephesians compares our faith to a shield. Just as a shield defends us against attacks, our faith does the same. Often this happens at a subconscious level, where the Word of God we have already consumed works on our behalf, blocking and diminishing any negative thoughts we are unaware of that are having an impact on our lives.

Nightmares

A beast with the body of a bear, the neck of a giraffe, and the face and teeth of a shark is chasing you. As you run, pure terror fills your heart as you realize that you are running toward the edge of a cliff. Do you face the monstrous beast that may rip you apart, or do you risk it all and jump off the ledge? Suddenly, you wake up sweating, your heart pounding. It seemed so real, but you realize that it was just a dream, a terrible nightmare. Thankfully, the beast was not real! Yet you still awoke feeling perturbed, and a gloomy feeling lingers.

According to the American Academy of Sleep Medicine, "An estimated 50% to 85% of adults report having the occasional nightmare."[1] *Merriam-Webster* defines a *nightmare* as "a frightening dream that usually awakens the sleeper."[2] Nightmares are dreams that originate from the demonic realm and bring fear, panic, and/or great anxiety to the dreamer. The activity within such a dream is often threatening and is always unpleasant. A person who has a nightmare may be scared enough to awaken from sleep screaming, kicking, and even fighting, with heart racing. A very vivid nightmare may also cause a person to have difficulty falling back asleep.

Medical researchers often relegate nightmares to being caused by such natural phenomena as lack of proper rest, the effects of drug abuse, sleep disorders, or stress. These elements may factor into the cause of nightmares, but the source is demonic activity. A study of the word *nightmare* sheds further light on its true origin. *Merriam-Webster* also defines *nightmare* as "an evil spirit formerly thought to oppress people during sleep."[3] One online article on the history of nightmares tells us, "The *Oxford English Dictionary* traces the first use of 'nightmare' in English to around 1300, as 'a female spirit or monster supposed to settle on and produce a feeling of suffocation in a sleeping person or animal.'"[4]

Sleep Paralysis, or Not?

Many individuals who have experienced intense nightmares have reported being unable to move their body parts or arise from their bed on awakening. Medical researchers attribute this phenomenon of sleep paralysis to factors such as poor blood circulation, sleep apnea, or narcolepsy. I do believe these factors can be contributors to natural sleep paralysis. However, when sleep paralysis is accompanied by nightmares, trepidation, and the awareness of an oppressive spiritual force, I strongly believe that a demonic spirit is at work.

As a child and young adult, I experienced this peculiar condition several times myself. I recall each time trying to cry out for help, but being unable to speak forth. My spirit man would instantly recognize the need to call upon the Lord Jesus, but it would sometimes take some seconds for me to be able to get His holy name out of my mouth. Every time this happened, the unseen attack would break immediately at the sound of the name *Jesus*. There is power in the name of Jesus! As I grew in the knowledge of the Word of God and my authority in Christ, these attacks stopped completely. As Jesus told us in Luke 10:19, "Behold, I give you the authority to trample on serpents and scorpions, and over all the power of the enemy, and nothing shall by any means hurt you."

Over the years, many have personally shared with me their own terrifying encounters in nightmares. They all related that their experience felt as if some invisible force or being was attempting to hold them down to the bed or strangle them. When I was younger, I heard some older people describe this experience as "a hank" (a hold) or "a hag riding a person's back." God has allowed me to pray for several individuals who were being constantly tormented by this type of experience, and they were freed from its force by the power of prayer.

Children and Nightmares

Up until the age of 22, rarely would I sleep without a nightlight or some type of light source nearby. As a child, I experienced several grueling nights where multiple nightmares tormented me. Some of these nights, the horrible dreams would be accompanied by demonic activity in my bedroom, such as hearing my name whispered or seeing a glimpse of shadows moving around within the room. A few times, I mustered enough courage to leave my bedroom and jump into my parents' bed. Many times, I shared these experiences with my parents. Their common response was, "It's just a bad dream; go back to sleep."

As a young adult, I wouldn't sleep or pray in the dark due to the many terrifying occurrences I experienced as a kid. There are many children who experience demonic dreams and night terrors and feel helpless. The enemy knows that children are easy targets and are often vulnerable to these types of attacks. Parents who are not spiritually mature brush off or oversimplify these dream encounters that their children experience.

Instead, if any of your children have been reporting nightmares, teach them to exercise authority in the name of Jesus Christ. Also advise them to flip on the lights in the room or keep a night-light on. Demons prefer darkness and secrecy. It's also important for you as an adult to announce your presence and declare out loud that any bad spirits are unwelcome. Command the spirits in Jesus' name to leave your child alone. Consecrate your child's room to God by anointing the door and windows with oil, while inviting the presence of the Holy Spirit to seal the room off from any demonic activity. My wife and I have used this method with success. Our four children have experienced very few nightmares or bad dreams.

Horror Movies and Social Media

The Bible admonishes us in Philippians 4:8 (KJV) with a prescription for what to think about and meditate on if we desire to maintain our position of peace and purity:

> Finally, brethren, whatsoever things are true, whatsoever things are honest, whatsoever things are just, whatsoever things are pure, whatsoever things are lovely, whatsoever things are of good report; if there be any virtue, and if there be any praise, think on these things.

Obviously, horror movies don't fit the criteria outlined in Philippians. Some horror movies serve as a tool for demonic encroachment into our lives. Many of the screenwriters are individuals who have not received salvation. Unbeknownst to them, they are open to being used by evil spiritual forces to bring imagery sourced from the demonic realm onto the big screen. Many individuals, especially children or adults more prone to fear, report an inability to fall asleep, night terrors, nightmares, or sudden battles with anxiety after watching some of these grotesque movies.

Once, at a church service at Dominion Ministries in Hampton, Virginia, the Lord had me call out a prophetic word that there was a young girl present who was being tormented by a demonic spirit. The Lord allowed me to describe the facial features of the evil being and that the young girl would see the spirit both in her dreams and during waking hours. In response, a mother came to the altar with her daughter clinging to her side. The daughter was weeping and looked oppressed by fear and anxiety.

At the altar, this mother shared with us that her daughter had attended a youth camp where she had accepted a dare from several youths. The dare involved watching a creepy social media video of a specific evil entity and calling out its name several times. This challenge seemed like innocent fun until a few days later, when the young girl began to see the wicked entity in her dreams. The entity began to harass, taunt, and attack the young girl in nightmares.

Night after night, this being would visit this girl in her dreams. As fear gripped her soul, the entity gained greater access into her life. The young girl began to see the demonic power in her room even while she was playing during the day. This constant barrage of evil caused her to experience great anxiety, a fear of being alone, and many sleepless nights. As soon as the spirit was rebuked in Jesus' name, however, the power of God came upon both the mother and daughter, freeing the family from the demonic spirit's wicked reign. The mother testified weeks later that all the attacks had ended and that her daughter's peace had returned to her.

We must be watchful over what activities we engage in, and especially what our children are exposed to. Ephesians 4:27 instructs not to "give place to the devil." Although a person may, through innocence or ignorance, give room to the enemy in his or her life, the power of Jesus Christ is able to prevail over the enemy. Better yet, however, it is wiser for us to follow the principles of the Word of God and not allow the enemy access in the first place.

Phobias

Love and fear are two very powerful feelings that engender strong emotional responses and often provoke a psychological response within individuals. Love tends to move us toward a more optimistic attitude, a better mental state, and a feeling of emotional pleasantry. In contrast, fear provokes pessimism, anxiety, and feelings of negativity. This is one of the reasons the Bible encourages us in 2 Timothy 1:7 that "God has not given us a spirit of fear, but of power and of love and of a sound mind."

God warns us against allowing a spirit of fear to grasp our souls and minds. Fear is a major door through which demonic forces enter into our thoughts and lives. While faith pleases God (see Hebrews 11:6), fear attracts the voice of the enemy. Any atmosphere infused with fear is usually one where confusion, division, and anxiety exists. This holds true in a workplace, a city, a household, or at an individual level in our own soul.

Fear can be a motivating factor for bad dreams, especially if fear has grown in our lives to the degree of becoming a phobia. One online dictionary defines a phobia this way: "an intense, persistent, irrational fear of a specific object, activity, situation, or person that manifests in physical symptoms such as sweating, trembling, rapid heartbeat, or shortness of breath, and that motivates avoidance behavior."[5]

The American Psychiatric Association (APA) recognizes that there exists a plethora of phobias, which the APA groups into three general categories: social phobias, agoraphobia, and specific phobias.[6] Many phobias that plague individuals are very rare and highly specific. For instance, anthophobia is a fear of flowers. Bibliophobia is a fear of books. These may seem silly and strange, but they do exist. I believe whenever there is a phobia involved, there may be a "spirit of fear" at work. This spirit can only be overcome by the Word and Spirit of God.

Although not all bad dreams result from demonic forces or influences, some bad dreams are the result of deep fears and phobias that may exist within our lives. People with a phobia or spirit of fear attached to their lives often experience recurring dreams. The recurring dreams are often about the thing that they fear happening to them. The enemy uses this tactic to further reinforce the stronghold of fear in a person's psyche.

One day while I was in prayer, the Lord spoke to me about a certain young lady whom I will call Janice for the sake of anonymity. The Lord said, "She is being abused by an incubus spirit." An incubus is a demon with a male identity that sexually attacks individuals (most often women) in their sleep. The targeted person may be awakened from sleep after experiencing perverted sexual dreams, unnatural feelings of arousal, someone on top of them, or even worse, an attempted penetration. The person awakens to find no physical person present, but often discerns that an invisible entity has attempted to molest him or her. If undealt with, the incubus spirit makes the person feel unclean and ashamed, and slowly zaps away his or her faith.

When I called Janice, I asked her if she had recently experienced an incubus attack. She responded yes and told me the attacks had been frequent.

"How frequent?" I asked.

I expected Janice to reply something like every few months. Instead, she responded, "A few times per week."

Janice was a believer in God, but somehow had allowed herself to fall into a place of being constantly harassed and oppressed by this demonic power in her dreams. I asked her if she had prayed against the attacks or had used her spiritual authority to overcome them. She replied that she had done neither. I instructed her to take authority over the incubus attack the next time it happened.

Janice made this attempt, but because her faith had slowly diminished over time, it was futile and only provoked the spirit further. The night she tried it, the incubus that had been attacking her only in her dreams now appeared as an apparition in her room and attempted to curse and choke her. It is important as believers in Jesus Christ that we immediately exercise our spiritual authority afforded to us through the Word of God whenever the enemy rears his ugly head. God has given us spiritual tools and keys within Scripture to help with this task, such as binding and loosing. In Matthew 18:18 Jesus says, "Assuredly, I say to you, whatever you bind on earth will be bound in heaven, and whatever you loose on earth will be loosed in heaven." I believe that had Janice released her faith immediately and put the Word to work on her behalf before the enemy could place her into captivity, she would have experienced liberty. She had knowledge of God's Word, but she didn't use it in a timely fashion and became a captive. We are admonished in James 1:22 to "be doers of the Word, and not hearers only."

After speaking with Janice, I came to realize how this demonic spirit had gained access to her soul. As a child, she had grown up in a household where her stepfather was a source of great aggravation for both Janice and her siblings. He was often angry, verbally abusive, and intimidating. There was always the fear in Janice that he might try to abuse her sexually as well. She felt unprotected by her mother, who was dealing with her own traumas and issues. Janice's constant fear of molestation opened a door for a phobia to set in and a spirit of fear to harass her.

The day after Janice unsuccessfully attempted to resist the incubus spirit, she reported its spiritual retaliation to me. My wife and I intervened on Janice's behalf. We both prayed over her, rebuked the dream attacks, and bound the incubus spirit in the name of Jesus Christ. That night, God gave Janice a dream indicative of her new freedom. In the dream, she saw a darkened sky filled with horrific-looking clouds. It was as if the clouds had grimacing faces. Suddenly, a bright light shone, the darkness fled, and the evil clouds vanished. Janice knew this dream was a supernatural sign from God. The perverted dream attacks, which had lasted six months, immediately ended, thanks to the power of the Holy Spirit.

Summary

As a loving Father, our God desires to speak to us in the night through dreams and nighttime prophetic encounters. His intentions are always to reveal His plans for our life and His great love for us, and to encourage us to fulfill our destiny. In contrast, the enemy of our soul, Satan, seeks to infiltrate our dream life to sow seeds of fear, discord, confusion, and anxiety. Jesus admonished His disciples in Matthew 26:41, "Watch and pray . . ." We must be discerning and watchful for these types of demonic dreams. If bad dreams and nightmares do appear in our lives, we must be prepared to respond by exercising our spiritual authority over the works of the enemy. Through the Word and the Holy Spirit, God has given us tools at our disposal that we can use to overcome all the trickery of the kingdom of darkness.

QUESTIONS FOR REFLECTIONS

1. How does Jesus' parable of a farmer having an enemy sow tares into his field relate to Satan and dreams?

2. How does watching horror movies or frightening social media content violate God's instruction found in Philippians 4:8? In what ways have you noticed how the things you watch or read can affect your dream life?

3. What are some Scriptures you can share with your children to help them exercise authority over bad dreams?

4. How can fears and phobias affect your dream life? Knowing that God hasn't given us a spirit of fear, but of power and love and a sound mind, what can you do about it?

six

The God Kind of Dreams

The psalmist King David reveals to us in Psalm 139:17 an attribute of God's nature in respect to humankind: "How precious also are Your thoughts to me, O God! How great is the sum of them!" The New Living Translation of this verse reads, "How precious are your thoughts about me, O God. They cannot be numbered!" God thinks about us daily. Our life, well-being, and destiny are always in the mind of God. This Scripture reveals to us that these thoughts are both precious and numerous. God's thoughts about us are so numerous that they cannot be numbered!

When we think about an individual, it often causes us to reach out and communicate with that person. This principle holds true for God as well. God not only thinks about us, but also continuously desires to communicate with us. One of the ways He conveys His heart, desires, and thoughts to us is through the dream realm. Not all dreams originate from God, but those that do are of great value and significance to us.

As we saw in chapter 2, the Lord promised in Joel 2:28, "And it shall come to pass afterward that I will pour out My Spirit on all flesh; your sons and your daughters shall prophesy, your old men shall dream dreams, your young men shall see visions."

One of the defining earmarks of our current dispensation of grace is the outpouring of the Holy Spirit upon all believers. Within this outpouring is the prophetic promise that visions and dreams will be released in abundance. The ability to receive from God in the visionary and dream realm is no longer just for the priest, prophet, and king, but is part of our divine inheritance as believers.

Most of us have already received dreams from God, whether we realize it or not. In the previous chapters, we discussed how to discern dreams where the source is either the soulish inside us or the demonic realm. In this chapter, we will discuss how you know if God is speaking to you in your dreams. I have taught individuals around the world the following seven rules of thumb that have helped them discern when it is God speaking in their dreams: (1) *the way a dream aligns with the Word of God*, (2) *the way a dream impacts our soul*, (3) *the way a dream links to our life*, (4) *the way a dream awakens us for prayer*, (5) *the way a dream brings healing*, (6) *the way a dream reveals truths about God*, and (7) *the way a dream brings hope*. Let's look more closely at each of these seven ways that we can discern whether God is speaking to us in a dream.

1. The way a dream aligns with the Word of God

The Word of God is our standard and foundation of faith as believers. Also, it is the perfect ruler or measuring stick for helping us determine if a dream, vision, or prophecy is from the Lord. A dream from God will align with the Word of God. Many people have been duped by false doctrines, New Age teachings, and the spirit of error because they lacked a knowledge of God's Word. It's very important that we weigh every spiritual experience, including our spiritually significant dreams, against Scripture.

Psalm 138:2 says, "For you have magnified Your word above all Your name." This Scripture reveals to us that God Himself will not contradict or go against His own words. Any revelation from the Holy Spirit, who inspired the Word of God, will always align with scriptural truths. The enemy will often attempt to exploit the ignorance of people who are not skilled in rightly dividing the Word of God.

A young woman named Clara has a dream in which she believes God instructed her to visit a psychic. The next day, while driving through her town, she sees a small office building with the sign "Psychic Mrs. Julia." The building looks exactly like the psychic office she saw in her dream and has identical signage. Clara becomes convinced that her dream was supernatural in nature and wonders if she is being led to this psychic for guidance and counsel.

To an unbeliever or new believer, this dream may appear to be God's divine providence. But a student of the Word of God would instantly recognize the hand of the enemy at play. The Bible discourages and in fact bans believers from dabbling in any occult practices or psychic arts. Deuteronomy 18:10–12 (KJV) says this:

> There shall not be found among you any one that maketh his son or his daughter to pass through a fire, or that useth divination, or an observer of times, or an enchanter, or a witch. Or a charmer, or a consulter with familiar spirits, or a wizard, or a necromancer. For all that do these things are an abomination unto the LORD.

Psychics operate through "familiar spirits." Familiar spirits are demonic spirits that attach themselves to people, places, and things and become familiar with them. They also connect themselves to family bloodlines and help enforce generational curses. Many psychics purport to deal with angelic beings, ancestors, or the spirit of a dead relative. However, these are familiar spirits that supply the psychics with detailed information about past events in people's lives. Psychics communicate with these spirits to gain information and supernatural knowledge.

However, it is sinful and unlawful to deal with these types of demonic forces. These demonic powers may give information, but they also open the door for calamity, deception, and other forms of evil. Accessing or relying on these dark powers means that a person is not dependent on God, but on His sworn enemy, Satan, the devil. God has blessed us with a better guide, His precious Holy Spirit, who only operates in truth and has our best interests in mind.

In the example with Clara and the psychic, the enemy attempted to deceive her into believing that her dream was from God. If she had given in to this deception, demonic doors could have been opened in her life and she would have been led down a dark path of falsehood. Instead, Clara's past exposure to solid Bible teachers and preachers had given her an understanding that God forbids psychic readings. She soon discerned that her dream did not align with Scripture, but rather was one of the "wiles of the devil" mentioned in Ephesians 6:11. She was able to repent concerning any doors of sin in her life and family bloodline that might have allowed the enemy access to try to lead her astray. The Bible warns that dealing with such occultic activities brings spiritual defilement into a person's life. Leviticus 19:31 (KJV) warns, "Regard not them that have familiar spirits, neither seek after wizards, to be defiled by them."

God would never give a revelation or guidance within a dream that would contradict His written Word and ordinances. So always ask yourself, *Does this dream align with the Word of God?* This first test of judging if a dream is a God dream is the simplest, yet most important. Reject and denounce any dreams that conflict with biblical truths and principles.

2. The way a dream impacts our soul

One of the things I love about dreams that proceed from God is the impact they have on our soul. The God kind of dreams leave an indelible impression in one's mind. Often, our subconscious is marked with the wisdom and counsel of God through these types of heavenly dreams. In simple terms, a dream from God carries more weight than a soulish dream.

The great Babylonian king Nebuchadnezzar experienced dreams from God, and we read in Daniel 2:3 (KJV) about the impact this had on his soul: "And the king said unto them, I have dreamed a dream, and my spirit was troubled to know the dream." The dreams this king received from God affected him so much that he was stirred up to try to figure out the meaning. God's dreams often provoke us to seek out the interpretation of what He is attempting to say to us.

Many individuals have contacted me about dreams that they knew were from God but they had no idea about the meaning. Although their dreams were often clouded with symbolism, they knew God was making an attempt to communicate some important truth to them. Many of the interpretations of these dreams are life changing and mind-blowing. Although a dream leaves an impact on our soul, we have the responsibility to seek God for the interpretation. King Nebuchadnezzar called for all his wise men to help him understand what message God was speaking to him in the night.

God has called us as "kings and priests unto God" (Revelation 1:6 KJV). Our kingly anointing gives us grace and favor to access the King of kings, the Lord Jesus Christ, for answers and understanding. Proverbs 25:2 tells us, "It is the glory of God to conceal a matter, but the glory of kings is to search out a matter." When you don't understand what God is revealing through a dream, take the time and make the effort to pray, meditate, and ask the right questions of God. He is faithful to give you the answers you seek.

3. The way a dream links to our life

Another important key to determining if dreams emanate from God is the link or relevancy a dream has to your life. As

I stated previously, many dreams are the result of the business and activities of life. These types of dreams often have garbled information and lack any relevance to our current season. I don't necessarily discard these dreams, but I don't give them as much attention as dreams that speak into the season of life I am in or the prayers I am currently praying.

God's dreams most commonly speak into our current season or the current issues that are weighing on our hearts. Once, I had a very complex work project that was due to be completed soon. This particular project had such attention focused on it from my superiors that it caused me a great deal of grief even to think about it. One night, I had a dream that I was trapped under a huge, supersized computer. The computer was the size of the old IBM mainframes that were larger than six-by-three-foot cabinets. Suddenly, a giant hand lifted the computer off me and flung it away. I knew that the dream was God's way of telling me that He was lifting the thoughts about this project that were weighing me down off my mind. I also knew that God would give me grace to complete the project successfully. After this dream, several co-workers volunteered to help me, and I was able to finish the task successfully. I also received an award and commendation for an excellent job done.

Too often, believers have shared dreams with me that speak directly into their challenges within their lives, but they ignore the significance of these dreams. God is trying to tell you something when a dream aligns with things that are already present in your life. Don't throw these dreams to the side or discard them. God is giving them to you for a reason, to help you on your life journey.

4. The way a dream awakens us for prayer

God dreams awaken us for prayer. Once, I fell asleep on my living room sofa and God gave me a dream about a young man from my former neighborhood who was in some type of

86

trouble. I got up and knelt by the sofa to pray for him. I fell back asleep, and God gave me a second dream about the same young man, showing me more of the troubled situation he was in and how he had landed himself in this trouble. I awoke a second time and briefly prayed for him again. A third dream was given to me that same night. This time, God showed me that if a supernatural intervention didn't take place, this young man would be killed by someone whom he had robbed. I saw in the dream the exact location where he would be killed. After this third dream, I leaped off the couch, fell to my knees, and pleaded for his life. A few days later, I made some calls to my hometown and made inquiries about the young man. The police had just arrested him on some petty charges. I knew that God had allowed this to happen to him to get him off the streets so that his life might be spared.

Often, an atmosphere of emotional intensity accompanies dreams where God is desirous of our urgent prayer. We may even feel agitated or uneasy until after we pray through the full burden of the Lord concerning a dream. In contrast, an emotional atmosphere of joy or excitement may accompany a dream that is revealing a blessing God wants to release into someone's life. God is simply looking for us to join our faith with heaven to see this blessing released.

When we awaken after a God-given dream, often our spirit is eager to know the meaning of the dream. Much of the communication from God in a dream isn't direct, but is embedded into the dream's symbolism. The abstract nature of dreams requires that we seek God for the interpretation and understanding. Sometimes, it's not only our own dreams from God that may stir us to pray, but also the dreams of others. This is what happened in the case of Nebuchadnezzar's prophetic dream. It was not the king himself, but rather Daniel and his friends who were ignited to seek God for answers. Daniel 2:16–18 says,

So Daniel went in and asked the king to give him time, that he might tell the king the interpretation. Then Daniel went to his house, and made the decision known to Hananiah, Mishael, and Azariah, his companions, that they might seek mercies from the God of heaven concerning this secret . . .

Oftentimes, when I receive a dream and I'm unsure about the full meaning, I do what Daniel did with his companions. I have a circle of close friends whom I contact to solicit their help. As we each contribute our insights into what God may be saying through the dream, a clearer picture is presented of God's intended communication.

At times, God gives us dreams that require we pray for understanding, but a dream may also require some intercession in order to be fulfilled in real life. Years ago, God repeatedly showed me in my dreams a very close relative worshiping God with us in church, even though this particular relative rarely went to church and had expressed no interest in attending any of my meetings. For several years, I had been decreeing that these dreams would manifest in real life. A few years ago, I was onstage ministering at one of our larger prophetic gatherings when one of my team members motioned for my attention and passed me a handwritten note. I looked at the note and realized that only one person could have written it—the one relative I had been given dreams about. I lifted my eyes and looked over to see this relative in the left corner section, waving at me. I had not invited this person but found out later that this particular relative had felt led to attend after hearing somewhere about the meetings. Since that time, this same relative has joyfully attended several of our meetings, has praised God with us, and has been touched by the presence of the Holy Spirit.

The God kind of dreams reveal to us the potentiality of what He can do in the natural. It is important that we exercise our faith and the power of prayer to partner with these dream revelations and release God's will in our lives and on the earth. Understanding this is especially important for intercessors who are called to war for lives and communities through fervent prayer. One of the keys for knowing when a dream requires you to seek the prayer partnership of other believers is checking your heart to see if a measure of faith is present to pray for the dream to become a reality. God often supernaturally deposits this new measure of faith in conjunction with dreams and visions that He shows us. Yet it can also help to bring other intercessors alongside you in praying for a God dream to become a reality.

5. The way a dream brings healing

God dreams bring healing. At our recent Parousia Encounter in Atlanta, Georgia, we experienced a deluge of God's glory. Many of the people in attendance testified to having supernatural encounters with God. One of the testimonies that struck a particular chord with me came from a pastor's wife. During the service, she felt the Lord Jesus Christ stand beside her, embrace her, and speak powerful, life-changing words to her. The Lord spoke, *The baby is with Me in heaven!*

These words made this pastor's wife break and come to tears. Just a few months before, she had experienced an unexpected pregnancy and an even more unexpected miscarriage. The miscarriage had brought heartache and disappointment, but she and her husband were able to overcome their grief. However, the Lord knew that there was a deeper level of healing needed within her soul. She didn't realize until after that encounter with God that there was still some residual grief from the loss of the baby. This woman of God's story stirred up my memory about another woman that I heard testify at a service years ago. This particular woman and her husband had been frustrated because throughout their years of marriage, they had been unable to have kids. To compound their agitation, they had suffered the heartbreak of multiple miscarriages. The prospect of ever having a child seemed hopeless. One night, the wife had a dream that seemed more like a real encounter to her. In the dream, the Lord Jesus took her into a place in heaven. She looked and saw several small kids in the distance, quite a ways off from the Lord. The Lord said to her, *Don't worry about your children. They are with Me in heaven. I will give you others.*

This woman awoke from that dream crying tears of healing and joy. She soon discovered that the Lord had supernaturally removed her heaviness, shame, and self-blame over her inability to have children. She and her husband were also soon able to testify that God had changed their situation and had enlarged their family.

6. The way a dream reveals truths about God

Over the years, I have had many dreams from God that gave me greater insights about His Word and Person. These kinds of dreams are some of the most fascinating and exciting. They help us gain insight into the things of God that we couldn't possibly comprehend with our own natural understanding. Supernatural God dreams help us "grow in the grace and knowledge of our Lord and Savior Jesus Christ," as 2 Peter 3:18 states.

Mahesh Chavda has a powerful prophetic ministry gift. He has evangelized in many nations and has won nearly a million souls to the Lord Jesus Christ. His ministry has been noted for powerful supernatural deliverances, healings, signs, and breakthroughs. Before he was an ardent believer in Christ and the Bible, Mahesh was a follower of the Hindu faith and an idol worshiper. One day in 1962 changed his life, however. While he was visiting a Hindu family who were his friends, a Baptist missionary knocked on their door and asked for a cup of water. Mahesh handed her the cup of water, and she handed him a Bible. He had never read the Bible or believed in Jesus the Christ, but the Bible intrigued him, and he began to read its stories and the Gospel message it contained.

Despite what Mahesh read in the Bible, it was challenging for him to accept Christ as his Lord. A confession of Christ and a departure from Hinduism would mean ridicule, persecution, and being shunned by his Hindu family and friends. Also, he would lose any influence or status that he possessed within the Hindu community. Accepting the Gospel truth would mean a departure from all that he had previously held dear.

God would use a powerful supernatural dream, however, to convince Mahesh that the Bible is real, that God is real, and that Jesus' love was beckoning him. In his book *The Hidden Power of Prayer and Fasting*, Mahesh described what happened in his dream:

Suddenly I went to sleep. I wasn't knocked on the head, nor did I drift off to sleep. This was something out of the ordinary. All of a sudden my head dropped down on the table and I was instantly taken to a place where I'd never been before. I was walking on streets of gold and I heard the most beautiful voices rising up in harmonies, singing songs, I'd never heard before. I saw colors I'd never seen before. I was in perfect ecstasy (which means a lot in Hindu!).

There was perfection all around me, but suddenly it all faded into insignificance when I saw the Source of perfection walking toward me. I saw a light brighter than 10,000 suns put together, yet it did not hurt my eyes. He came toward me, and somehow I knew that He was the person of Jesus. I'll never forget His eyes. When I looked into their depths, it was as if He had felt every pain in the world and had shed every tear that had ever been shed on earth. Pure love shone from His eyes in perfect combination with victory and triumph. Then He came and put His hands on my shoulders and said, "My little brother. . . ."[1]

7. The way a dream brings hope

God dreams not only have the ability to bring healing and revelation to our hearts, but also hope to our souls. While I was ministering at Renew Life Worship Center in Woodbridge, Virginia, the leaders there, Bishop Bennet Aboagye and his wife, apostle Dr. Gina Aboagye, shared a powerful personal testimony with me. Here is an excerpt that relates their testimony, adapted from their book *At the Appointed Time:*

> Ever since we met, we have been madly in love. After our marriage we lived in Accra-Ghana for two years, and later migrated to the United States. During that time, we consistently attempted to have a child, but unfortunately we could not and constantly ended up miscarrying. After over eighteen miscarriages, some of which were twins, our hearts were shuttered at the loss of so many lives, but our faith in God and His Word sustained us.
>
> We never gave up, but kept trusting a word God Almighty had spoken to us in regard to the promise of a son. During this phase while we were subject to infertility, we both traveled to countless countries across the globe merely to visit different doctors. We visited over twenty specialists all around the globe. The Word of God and the power of prayer kept us going and helped us to stay strong. We endured a lot of ridicule, shame, scorn and rejection only because we could not bear a child, and were labelled as *"Barren."*[2]

Although the Aboagyes experienced more than eighteen heart-wrenching miscarriages, God gave them many supernatural dreams and prophetic words to help them persevere. They allowed the revelations God gave them about a son to anchor their hope. They were eventually able to have their first child, a baby boy named Evidence! Their testimony has reached many people and changed many lives.

Dreams from God allow us to see in the spirit realm what hasn't been seen yet in the natural. Our physical circumstances may say one thing to our five senses, but our spirit man (or woman) can see beyond the now, into the future, through dreams and visions God gives us. Romans 8:25 (KJV) tells us, "But if we hope for that we see not, then do we with patience wait for it." Where there is hope, there is patience and an expectation that God will show Himself strong on our behalf.

Years ago, I was in dire financial straits. Having extra money at the time was more rare for me than seeing the Queen of England walking down Fifth Avenue in New York. I had sought God heavily about the matter and pleaded with Him for breakthrough, but I heard nothing from the Holy Spirit concerning my situation. I would speak to God about my money problems, and He would speak to me about a situation another person was having. Often, He would instruct me to pray for that person or go to him or her with a prophetic answer to a dilemma.

Over time, it became discouraging that God had little to say to me about my own situation and a lot to say to me about other people and what they were facing. One day, I decided to lie down on my couch to take a nap. As soon as I had lain down, I had a dream. The dream was unusual because it seemed to be in slow motion. It was one of only two dreams I have ever had in slow motion. I believe God wanted to really get my attention. In the dream, I saw hundred-dollar bills with Benjamin Franklin's face on them floating past my eyes. Six or seven of these hundred-dollar bills floated by slowly, and then the dream ended.

When I awoke, I knew God was saying to me through the symbolism in the dream that He had heard my prayers and was going to release resources to me. Over the next few weeks, I received phone call after phone call from individuals who gave me the same account of what happened. They would say, "For some reason, God placed you on my heart to give you this amount of money!" God proved His faithfulness, and He used one supernatural dream to encourage my faith that heaven was responding to my plea. Supernatural dreams from God often bring a response to your prayers that releases hope to you that your situation will change in your favor.

A Quick Word of Caution

When people have dreams that have a supernatural or prophetic tone, they are often eager to gain an understanding of the meaning of the dreams. As a result, many individuals purchase books or search online to gain further insight or an interpretation of their dreams. Some great resources are available on this topic, but I must also issue a warning: Not all of the authors and "experts" on dream interpretation are Christian or Holy Spirit-led. In fact, some are just the opposite, so it's important to be cautious.

It's important to be aware that some of the available resources on dream interpretation are written by New Age authors who are sharing information from a tainted, occultic perspective. Often, their interpretation of dreams and dream symbolism may directly contradict truths found within the Word of God. I have had to warn even well-meaning Christians about being prayerful and Spirit-led about what resources they access to gain a greater understanding of the dream realm. (In question 14 of the "Twenty Questions & Answers about Supernatural Dreams" section that concludes this book, I provide you with information on two Christian books that I recommend for further reference on understanding dream symbolism.)

Summary

God dreams allow us supernatural insight that encourages us and can help us, through prayer, to reverse the plans of the enemy and enforce the will of God on the earth. We must allow the Word of God to be our spiritual plumb line to help us weigh if a dream is from God. There are seven important rules of thumb that we can apply to help us understand whether a dream proceeds from God. These are (1) *the way a dream aligns with the Word of God*, (2) *the way a dream impacts our soul*, (3) *the way a dream links to our life*, (4) *the way a dream awakens us for prayer*, (5) *the way a dream brings healing*, (6) *the way a dream reveals truths about God*, and (7) *the way a dream brings hope*. All of these important factors should be taken into account. The God kind of dreams have the greatest potential to release destiny into the earth.

QUESTIONS FOR REFLECTION

1. Why should the revelation within the dreams you act on never contradict Scripture?

2. How do your feelings about a dream, or how a dream impacts your soul, help you determine if a dream is from God?

3. What type of sources, resources, and writers should you avoid when attempting to understand a dream? Why is this important?

4. Have you ever had a God dream that awakened you for prayer? What is one way to know that a dream requires that you ask others to partner with you in prayer?

seven

The Dream Compass

P eople from all walks of life have one thing in common: they need wisdom to handle the daily affairs of life. The more responsibility a person has in life, and the more influence he or she wields, the greater the need for wisdom and direction.

Proverbs 4:7 says, "Wisdom is the principal thing; therefore get wisdom. And in all your getting, get understanding." The Word of God admonishes us that we should pursue understanding and wisdom, especially the supernatural kind that stems from God.

That's where dreams and the dream compass come in. Supernatural dreams allow us a peek into the divine guidance of heaven and the wisdom of God.

God's Instrument

Merriam-Webster defines *compass* as "a device for determining directions by means of a magnetic needle or group of needles turning freely on a pivot and pointing to the magnetic north."[1] Compasses are instruments that sailors, pilots, geographers, and miners have used for years to help them navigate. In ancient

97

times especially, sailors relied on these devices, along with the celestial bodies, to help them plan and direct the route their ships would sail. God often uses dreams as a spiritual compass to help direct us on the routes we should take in life.

There is one need common to all of humankind, regardless of color or creed. That is the need for direction. We just saw in Proverbs 4:7 that wisdom is the principal thing we need to get. The wisdom of God helps us understand the proper course of action to take in every circumstance. A right or wrong decision in life can make the difference between finding favor or suffering heartache from failure.

Fortunately, God has promised us in James 1:5, "If any of you lacks wisdom, let him ask of God, who gives to all liberally and without reproach, and it will be given to him." What a wonderful promise! God loves to dish out wisdom and direction to us. Giving it without reproach means that God won't withhold wisdom from us due to our faults. We serve a merciful God. Often, He communicates direction and wisdom with us through the dream realm.

It's a Grand Affair

In the fall of 2009, my now-wife and I were looking for a venue to host our wedding ceremony. In our region there are many wonderful wedding venues, especially along the Virginia Beach oceanfront. We desired a location that could accommodate our guests, be visually appealing, serve good food, and be within our price range. We researched and visited a number of local facilities, hotels, and banquet halls.

One Thursday, we had an appointment scheduled for a venue called Grand Affairs in Chesapeake, Virginia. Grand Affairs sat on the rolling hills of a beautiful golf course and featured an elegant banquet hall with chandeliers, large glass windows, and pristine decor. And it was in a great location that would

98

be easily accessible for our local and out-of-town guests. I was elated to discover that the cost to host a summer wedding there was considerably lower than many of the other less-inviting places we had visited.

The sales representative was very pleasant, welcoming, and hospitable. She handed us the rental agreement and said it would only be $1,500 to secure the venue. It seemed like a steal of a deal. My fiancé and I were both excited that we had found a proper venue for our upcoming wedding. However, something inside me, which I now know was God, told me to wait. I advised the representative that we would be back on Monday with the funds to secure the banquet hall for the agreed-upon date.

That Sunday night, God gave me a short but clear dream. In the dream, I saw myself on the golf course of the Grand Affairs estate and heard one word loudly: *Wait!* Upon awakening, I shared with my frustrated wife-to-be that I would not be taking the cashier's check to the sales representative on Monday, but that I would wait.

I partially discerned the wisdom of God in this matter. When God told me to wait, I thought He meant wait another day before rendering the payment. So on Tuesday, Jessica and I both drove up to Grand Affairs to submit our check for deposit. Surprisingly, the office was closed in the middle of the day, and there was a sign on the door: *Closed for Business*. That day, we attempted several times to call the office, but there was no answer. Finally, we called their sister Grand Affairs site, and the management shared with us that the Chesapeake location had closed and was out of business.

Our minds raced. We were disappointed that our wedding would not be held at this gorgeous facility and that we would have to continue our search for a venue, but we were elated that God had saved us from heartache and financial loss. Had we paid our money on the previous Thursday, or even on Monday, we would have lost our deposit of $1,500.

That may not seem like a lot of money, but at that time, we were operating on a shoestring budget. If a person ever needs God's guidance, it's when planning a wedding on a shoestring budget. Actually, in those days my budget was more like just the string itself. I had a saying: "I'm as broke as a bag of glass!" Losing the $1,500 would have deflated our faith and set us back in our ability to secure a wedding venue. God's supernatural dream gave me just enough clarity to wait an extra day, which allowed me to avoid jeopardy.

Which Door to Walk Through

One of the challenges of being a sought-after international speaker is not the availability of speaking opportunities, but being certain to choose the God-given doors. In ministry, it's very important to be in the right place at the right time with the right people. This is one of the keys to experiencing the supernatural in one's life and ministry.

A few years ago, I had a very demanding travel schedule, coupled with working a full-time secular job. It was very challenging balancing both of those and our home life. I had to be very discerning and intentional about which doors to walk through and which to decline. Working a full-time job restricted me to only a limited number of days per year to travel.

One day, I was reviewing several international ministry invitations. That evening, I prayed and asked God which speaking engagement to accept. Early the next morning, God answered me through a very vivid prophetic dream in which I saw an African man standing in front of me and inviting me to Ireland. The dream reminded me of the experience that the apostle Paul had in Acts 16:9: "And a vision appeared to Paul in the night. A man of Macedonia stood and pleaded with him, saying, 'Come over to Macedonia and help us.'"

In the dream, I didn't recognize the face of the man and found it unusual that it would be an African man inviting me to Ireland. The next morning when I checked my inbox, I had received a written invitation from a dear Nigerian leader named Pastor Chuks in Dublin, Ireland, inviting me to come minister for a special program that he was hosting at his ministry. Earlier that year, I had met Pastor Chuks's wife, Sally, while visiting a friend's home. She had shared with her husband about my ministry, and while he was in prayer, God put in his spirit for him to invite me. I immediately answered yes to his invitation.

I had been uncertain about which assignment to accept, but God spoke to me in the night, giving me a clear and undeniable answer in my dream to my prayer request. Amazingly, when I had asked God which door was from Him, Ireland had not been on my radar. Yet when I visited Ireland for the first time, God worked many power healings and deliverances. I was also able to share that it was God who had sent me to the people there through a powerful dream revelation.

Many times in your life, when you are uncertain if you should say yes or no, accept or decline, or go left or right, pay attention to your dream content. The answer from God may lie within.

When Others Dream about You

Gideon was a servant of the Lord who lived in Israel during a time when it was oppressed and impoverished by the Midianites. In Judges 6:11–22, Gideon experiences a profound angelic visitation that stirs him up to destroy the altar of Baal and become a deliverer for Israel. After taking command of the army of Israel, he asks God for a supernatural sign as proof of His support for Gideon's mission:

> So Gideon said to God, "If You will save Israel by my hand as You have said—look, I shall put a fleece of wool on the threshing

floor; if there is dew on the fleece only, and it is dry on all the ground, then I shall know that You will save Israel by my hand, as You have said."

Judges 6:36–37

Gideon had experienced an amazing angelic encounter and a miraculous supernatural sign as God's approbation upon his life. However, God knew that Gideon needed further encouragement and direction concerning his military campaign against the Midianites. This green light would come in the form of a dream:

It happened on the same night that the LORD said to him, "Arise, go down against the camp, for I have delivered it into your hand."

Judges 7:9

God instructs Gideon to sneak into the camp of the Midianites at night and spy on them. Gideon probably thought he would uncover a weakness in their military formation, but no! God had set up for him to overhear a dream being spoken about:

And when Gideon had come, there was a man telling a dream to his companion. He said, "I have had a dream: To my surprise, a loaf of barley bread tumbled into the camp of Midian; it came to a tent and struck it so that it fell and overturned, and the tent collapsed."

Then his companion answered and said, "This is nothing else but the sword of Gideon the son of Joash, a man of Israel! Into his hand God has delivered Midian and the whole camp."

Judges 7:13–14

How elated Gideon must have been to hear that one of his opponents had had a dream that was interpreted as Midian's imminent defeat at the hands of Gideon. Overhearing the dream of this Midianite was the final motivation Gideon needed to spur him on to execute Israel's attack:

> And so it was, when Gideon heard the telling of the dream and its interpretation, that he worshiped. He returned to the camp of Israel, and said, "Arise, for the LORD has delivered the camp of Midian into your hand."
>
> Judges 7:15

God had given Gideon both an angelic visitation and a supernatural sign with a fleece, but it was a prophetic dream that gave him the courage to fully obey the Lord.

God may choose to answer our prayers for direction through a dream. However, as in Gideon's case, the answer, direction, or instruction may come in a dream that someone else has pertaining to us. There have been several times in my life that people have shared a dream God has given them with me in it. Although the dream may have seemed confusing or meaningless to the individual, often encoded within the dream's content was the very direction that I needed from God. It's important to discern not only how God is speaking to you through your own dreams, but also through the dreams of others.

You're Taking Him Where?

In 2013, I was invited to minister in Nigeria, a great nation in West Africa. Before this ministry excursion, my wife and I both fasted and prayed together for several days. During our time of prayer, God revealed that both my wife and my newborn son should accompany me to Nigeria. I was very hesitant to share this revelation with my wife, because I knew that as a mother she might feel apprehensive about our new son traveling with us to a nation reported to have high rates of kidnapping, terrorism, disease, and robbery.

When I shared with Jessica that I felt our son should travel with us instead of being left behind with a babysitter or family member, I thought she would ridicule such a notion. Surprisingly, she shared with me that while in prayer she also felt that we should take our son with us, but she was unsure why. She had been hesitant to share her own impression from God with me. We agreed that we would ask God for further clarity and confirmation on our decision. That night, God gave me a dream in which I saw our young son boarding an airplane with us to Africa. We felt this was the further prophetic confirmation we needed to solidify our final decision.

Although someone may feel strongly that he or she has heard from God, often challenges to one's faith still come. Our biggest adversity was the objection from our family members. Several close relatives prodded us with questions about how as "good parents" we could take our newborn into a troubled nation. Although our relatives had never visited Africa, news reports had convinced them that it was a dangerous venture. I was asked repeatedly, "You're taking him where?" and "How sure are you that this is the right decision?"

A few months later, my wife, our nine-month-old son, and I arrived on an Air France flight to Nigeria during the early evening hours. We were tired from the long flight but excited to tour the land and share the Gospel. Shortly after we departed the airport, a soldier stopped the vehicle we were in, which was being driven by our host. The soldier was manning a roadside checkpoint, and apparently our driver had angered him by passing the checkpoint without coming to an abrupt stop.

This soldier approached our vehicle very aggressively. His eyes were red, and his countenance was one of anger. I'm sure standing in the hot African sun all day added to his irritability. He berated our driver for speeding, and with a commanding presence told the driver to pull over to the side of the road. We looked to the side, and all we could see were bushes surrounding a ditch. This soldier was asking us in the dark night to park out of the view of anyone. The first thing that came to my mind were the many extrajudicial killings that allegedly took place, carried out by the military and police in Nigeria.

Out the back window, I could see that the soldier was holding a firearm that resembled a FN FAL machine gun. He commanded our driver to first roll down all the windows before pulling over near the bushes. When the soldier saw my young son in the car, he became even madder while exclaiming, *"You have a baby in the car! You have a baby in the car! I can't believe it!"*

This soldier was so disgusted that the driver was speeding with a baby in the car that he instructed us, *"Just go! Just go!"* We happily sped off to safety and continued on our journey.

"The foolishness of God is wiser than men," 1 Corinthians 1:25 states. It had seemed foolish to our relatives for us to take our young son on a journey to Nigeria. In His infinite foreknowledge, however, God used our obedience in bringing our son along to save us from trouble that only He knew was coming. We could have been imprisoned or assaulted by the demonized soldier if we had not had our son in the car with us. God used a dream as a compass to help us properly navigate making our decision about taking our son along. Doing so could very well have saved our lives.

Increasing Wisdom and Direction

God desires to give us supernatural wisdom and direction. It is very important for us to build our faith in regard to receiving from God. As our faith and expectancy increase for God to speak to us, there will also be an increase of wisdom-giving dreams. Meditating on Scriptures that pertain to God's guidance will cause your expectation to rise for Him to speak to you in this manner.

In 1 Samuel 13:14, God noted King David for being "a man after His own heart." I believe that King David possessed several attributes God commended. David was a man who had a heart of worship, humility, faith, forgiveness, courage, and repentance. Also, a notable character strength was that David had a great dependence upon God. As we study David's life, it is evident that he sought the Lord frequently for direction. This allowed him to achieve many successes and win many battles.

King David wrote in Psalm 16:7 (KJV), "I will bless the LORD, who hath given me counsel." He recognized that his anointing and victories were resultant of the Lord giving him counsel. He decided that it was important to record his worship and appreciation of the Lord as his spiritual guide. Also, in the second part of this same verse, King David shares a powerful truth with us from his life: "My reins also instruct me in the night seasons." Reins are long, often leather straps attached at one end of a horse's bit. They are used by a horse's rider to guide or stop the horse. King David was using figurative language to share how God can use the night hours' activity, which would include dreams, to guide us. Often, the message or content within a dream has the ability to turn our hearts concerning a decision we are about to make in life. King David compares this guiding ability of God and dreams in the night to a horse's rider using the reins to change the direction and movement of a horse.

There have been many times when God has given me, or someone close to me, a dream that totally changed the direction of a course of action. God knows obstacles, challenges, and things outside our ability to know. Because He is omniscient, His counsel is always absolutely reliable and in our best interests. Supernatural dreams help shift our spiritual reins so that we can learn to follow the leading of God more perfectly.

Summary

Dreams from God are often packaged with answers to the direction we should take or the decisions we should make in life. Unfortunately, too often individuals neglect the power of these instructions found within their dreams. This neglect of God's dream compass for us leads to unnecessary grief and failure. As children of God, we must always endeavor to follow the leading of the Holy Spirit. This leading may come to us through an internal impression, the voice of the Holy Spirit, or a dream given to us by God. Romans 8:14 tells us, "For as many as are led by the Spirit of God, these are sons of God." As you determine to be intentional about following the guidance that God releases to you in the dream realm, you will discover countless new victories in every area of life.

=========== **QUESTIONS FOR REFLECTION** ===========

1. What does the Bible say is the "principal thing" we must get? How can our dreams play a part in pursuing it?

2. What do a compass and a dream from God have in common?

3. When was the last time that you prayed to God to give you guidance through dreams? What happened as a result?

4. Have others had dreams about you that have impacted your life? Or have you had significant dreams that have impacted others?

eight

God's Alarm in the Night

In Joel 2:1, God says, "Blow the trumpet in Zion, and sound an alarm in My holy mountain! Let all of the inhabitants of the land tremble . . ." There are times when God greatly desires to get our attention, especially when grave matters are about to present themselves in our lives. The Holy Spirit has a unique way to sound an alarm in our spirit by speaking a word of warning and urgency to us in the night hours.

The inhabitants of Israel were trained to stop all their activity and "tremble" when the ram's horn alarm sound was blown. Warnings from God should grab hold of our attention and cause us to take some type of action. God uses dreams as part of His warning system for us. There have been many accounts of individuals receiving life-saving messages through dreams. Even unbelievers have benefited from these types of dreams. God is always interested in the well-being of humankind and uses whatever methods are available to communicate with His creation.

In this chapter, you will read biblical narratives of God using dreams to bring warning into the lives of the saints of old. Also, I will share some powerful personal accounts where God used dreams for divine intervention. As you read these stories, you will grow to understand that God has good plans and thoughts for us. He doesn't desire bad things to happen to us, and He often seeks to prevent negative events from happening in our lives. When we learn to listen to His voice and leading by discerning His supernatural messages while we sleep, we can be spared a lot of trouble in life.

No Shocker

When my son was eight years old, my wife had a dream with him in it. In the dream, he was playing in our kitchen and one of his toys rolled near one of the power outlets. For some reason, he realized that his toy had knocked an AC power adapter out of the wall. As he attempted to plug the adapter back in, he was electrocuted. The electrical charge from the socket knocked my young son to the floor in the dream.

Jessica had to call 9-1-1 for emergency medical help in the dream. She saw an ambulance pull up to our home and emergency medical personnel proceed to try to administer life-saving assistance to my son. She saw them wheel him away on a stretcher to a local hospital, where he would need to receive further medical treatment. As the dream ended, my wife was unable to see what ultimately happened to our son, but she knew he had been severely harmed.

Usually when one of us has a dream about something happening to the children, we take authority through prayer. As we pray, we cancel the plans of the enemy and decree the will of God. However, due to the business of life at the time, we didn't have a chance to pray about Jessica's dream. On the particular day after the dream, I was away traveling for a ministry assignment and she was busy taking care of the kids. While Jessica was in the kitchen preparing breakfast that morning, exactly what had happened in the dream began to play out in real life.

My son's toy went near the trash can and knocked the AC power adapter out of the socket. My wife leaped into action. God brought back to her remembrance the dream from just hours earlier. She was able to intercept our son before he could tamper with the electrical plug.

We believe that this intervention by God may well have saved our son's life. This particular outlet contained exposed wires that had been installed for the previous homeowner's unused alarm system. When my wife related to me how prophetic her dream had been, I praised God for His mercy. It is necessary that we take dreams about someone being harmed, especially about a loved one, very seriously.

As Jessica and I celebrated God's goodness, I was reminded of a very hope-inspiring passage of Scripture, Jeremiah 29:11: "For I know the thoughts that I think toward you, says the LORD, thoughts of peace and not of evil, to give you a future and a hope." God's thoughts toward us are for our well-being, and His intentions toward us are ones of peace and blessing. The enemy of our soul, Satan, loves to orchestrate moments to steal joy and peace from us, but God desires the opposite. I love what the NIV translation of this passage says about God having "plans to prosper you and not to harm you." God doesn't want us to be harmed!

A Baby Is Saved

Herod, who served as king of Judea, was used by Satan to try to destroy the plan of God to raise up a Savior for all of Israel and humankind. When Herod heard that wise men from the East had ventured to Jerusalem in search of the prophesied Messiah of the Jews, he became troubled and sought to dupe the wise men through trickery.

Herod feigned a desire to go and worship the child Messiah once the wise men would reveal to him the location of the child's birth. Herod's true desire, however, was to kill the newborn baby, ending not only the child's life, but the threat to Herod's own reign and rulership. His intentions were desperately wicked and demonically driven. He could be likened to other despots such as Hitler and Pol Pot, who became intoxicated by the power they wielded.

What happens next reveals the power of God-given dreams to deliver warnings that can save lives, stop the works of Satan, and preserve destinies. Matthew 2:12 (KJV) tells us of the wise men, "And being warned of God in a dream that they should not return to Herod, they departed into their own country another way." Herod's wicked intentions were made known to the wise men through a supernatural revelation God gave them in a dream. They were wise enough (no pun intended) to obey the voice of God and escape from Herod's evil grasp and influence.

An infuriated Herod then issued an edict of terror that all children two years and under in Bethlehem should be slain (see Matthew 2:16). But Jesus' stepdad, Joseph, had a dream in which he was forewarned by God of Herod's madness:

Now when they had departed, behold, the angel of the Lord appeared to Joseph in a dream, saying, "Arise, take the young Child and His mother, flee to Egypt, and stay there until I bring you word; for Herod will seek the young Child to destroy Him." When he arose, he took the young Child and His mother by night and departed for Egypt.

Matthew 2:13–14

God would not allow the eternal purposes that He had predestined through the life of the holy child Jesus to perish due to Herod's cunning. Instead, God activated His early alarm system in the life of Jesus' stepfather, Joseph. Fortunately for the baby Jesus and for all of humanity, Joseph did not scoff at or ignore the supernatural warning dreams given to him. When God gives us these types of dreams, we have the same responsibility as Joseph to respond wholeheartedly, with urgency and obedience.

Three Important Factors

Thankfully, Joseph heeded the angelic warning that allowed the life of baby Jesus to be preserved. His act of obedience was a contributing factor in the generations to come after him being able to receive forgiveness of sins, redemption, and salvation. Also, the dastardly plan of Satan through King Herod was thwarted.

This profound account in Matthew 2 reveals to us three important factors concerning warning dreams. First, sometimes God will use an angel to bring us a message within a dream. This is the methodology God used with Joseph. Angels are God's heavenly messengers who are "sent forth to minister for them who shall be heirs of salvation" (Hebrews 1:14 KJV). Who are the heirs of salvation? Those of us who have received King Jesus as our Lord and Savior are the heirs of salvation. Angels work as servants and messengers for us, to help us accomplish the will of God for our lives. Therefore, dreams where angels are sent to bring us communications from God truly take on a supernatural and prophetic nature!

Second, warning dreams often contain not only cautions, but instructions. Joseph was warned to flee Bethlehem. Also, he was told specifically to relocate to Egypt. The instructions contained within such dreams are often just as important as the warnings themselves. Failing to obey the instruction within a dream may cause you to miss a divine opportunity. Also, failure to heed a dream's instruction may cause you to be subjected to some form of woe or distress.

Third and last, warnings from God should be considered high priority and time sensitive. It's important to take heed to the warning and instruction, but also to do so in a timely fashion. These dreams often convey a sense of urgency that stirs one's soul to take action quickly. It can be risky to be negligent or slothful when God sends a supernatural warning of any kind. Imagine if Joseph had waited a few extra weeks to obey the warning the angel of God had given him in his dream. Herod could very well have captured him and his family in that time delay, holding them prisoner or subjecting them to physical harm. Failure to react to a God-given dream in a timely manner could cause you great grief or despair in life.

A Unique Children's Ministry

Not all prophetic warning dreams are intended as a deterrent for us directly. Many warning dreams from God are released to us to provoke us to intercession. As I mentioned in an earlier chapter, there have been many times when I have been suddenly awakened in the middle of the night. Immediately, a certain person's name would drop in my spirit, or the Holy Spirit would show me an individual's face. Instinctively, I would know that God desired for me to intercede for this person.

At times, the burden to intercede for someone can be so heavy upon you that it seems as if you are standing in the gap for that person. That's what it means to intercede. In Ezekiel 22:30 (KJV) God described it this way: "And I sought for a man among them, that should make up the hedge, and stand in the gap before me for the land, that I should not destroy it: but I found none." God issued a complaint to Ezekiel that there wasn't anyone interceding for the children of Israel. Also, it was both a challenge and an invitation to Ezekiel to assume the role and responsibility of intercessor for his nation.

As you read this, you may be remembering times when you have been awakened in the night, sometimes with a sense of urgency but still unsure of what to do. I suggest that you just start praying. Pray in your heavenly prayer language if you have received the baptism of the Holy Spirit. God will illuminate in your spirit what or who you are praying for or about. Many plans of the enemy have been stopped through intercession that was motivated by some type of warning dream sent to one of God's people.

Years ago when I pastored a small church in Virginia, God gave me a prophetic word for one of our members at the time. Her name was Monique, and the Lord said to her, *I will give you a ministry and burden for children.* Several of the other church members congratulated her on the prophetic word. Monique returned a most interesting response to the word of the Lord: "I don't want a children's ministry, and I don't enjoy working with kids."

The tonality of Monique's response caused our eyes to get big and our mouths to hang open. Her response also provoked a bit of laughter since we were not expecting those words from her. It wasn't that she didn't love kids. She just didn't enjoy doing kiddie activities. I told her, "Well, God may change your heart. I know that I heard this clearly from the Lord for you."

In my mind, Monique was going to be the woman in charge of our children's ministry. Yet God had a totally different plan. Suddenly, Monique began to have dreams about children. However, they weren't dreams about working with children within the church. Every dream was about a child in danger. God started frequently awakening her to pray about dire situations regarding kids. He would show her the situation in a dream, and then she would awaken with a heavy burden to pray.

I remember one dream where Monique saw a young boy who had been kidnapped and was being held captive. The kidnappers hid the young boy in an underground cellar in their backyard, which had a stone lid that they placed over the top. She shared this dream with us. We all prayed and believed God would free this young boy. Within days, she sent us the news report of a young boy who had been kidnapped and had been freed by the police after being held in this exact type of predicament.

Monique had several dreams of this type that were serious and intense in nature, all revolving around kids. Several times, we saw news reports that matched her dreams of kids being rescued. God gave her a special ministry to children, one where He would give her warning dreams about kids in peril. And then her intercession, we believed, would cause them to be rescued. God may have graced in you a certain area of warning dreams too. Maybe He has graced you to pray for marriages in trouble, schools that the enemy wants to target, churches, or a particular family member. It's important to take those dreams that prompt intercession on your part seriously, and remember what powerful things God can and will do in response to your prayerful obedience.

A Timely News Story

It's always exciting for me when I receive an invitation to share the Gospel in a nation I have never visited before. In 2015, a friend connected me with a bishop in Burundi that I really took a liking to. I believed greatly in this bishop's ministry. A few months after our first communication, he invited me to his homeland of Burundi to minister at a special leadership conference.

Anytime I receive an invitation to minister in a foreign nation, I pray about it. Also, I have my wife and prayer team seek the Lord for guidance. I was already aware that Burundi, much like other parts of Central Africa, was experiencing turmoil and political tension. However, it was not unusual for God to send me to troubled nations to bring hope with the Gospel message. During this particular season in my life, I was traveling to Africa a lot. I was elated at this new opportunity to share the Gospel.

My excitement about this new ministry door soon deflated after my wife shared a dream that God gave her. Jessica had prayed, specifically asking Him if it was His will for me to go to Burundi at that season in time. That same night, she had a very vivid dream where she saw the land of Burundi. In the dream, it was as if a giant pit of darkness opened up and swallowed the nation. Also, in the dream she could sense evil, chaos, and panic. Although I was not afraid to travel anywhere, I was not foolish enough to ignore this clear warning from God. I decided to ask the bishop if I could postpone my travel for a possible future date.

A few weeks later, an online news article appeared with the headline, "Burundi is 'Going to Hell' Says US Ambassador to United Nations."[1] The article detailed how a United Nations special envoy and a U.S. ambassador reported deadly violence, riots, and chaos within the nation. The U.S. State Department warned American citizens against traveling to Burundi and evacuated much of their own staff within the nation. Also, no UN peacekeeping forces were present to assist Westerners who might need protection within the nation.

My wife and I realized the significance of the dream God had given her weeks earlier, and that God had protected me by preventing my travel to this nation. Had I accepted the invitation, I possibly could have been trapped within the nation or been subjected to victimization, and I could have lost the financial investment required to travel for missions trips. It is important that we allow God's alarm of caution within our dreams to override our own emotions and desires.

Summary

God often gives us prophetic dream warnings as preemptive measures against the dastardly plans of the enemy. We must take these types of dreams very seriously and heed them in a timely manner. Often embedded within warning dreams are specific instructions from God that help us understand not only what to avoid, but what we should do next. Also, being forewarned of God in a dream is one proof of God's love and mercy toward us. Sadly, I have seen too many individuals ignore very clear and concise dreams from God about an action they should not take or a door they should not walk through. Almost always without fail, they suffered some form of great mishap or tragedy that could have been avoided if only they had opened their hearts to God and had yielded to the supernatural directives He gave them. When taken seriously, warnings that are supernatural in nature release God's supernatural protection on your behalf. God has a myriad of ways to give us warnings, but supernatural dreams play a major role in His alarm system.

=== QUESTIONS FOR REFLECTION ===

1. What is a biblical example of someone being forewarned in a dream? What have you learned that you can apply in your own life from this example?

2. Why are warning dreams often more time sensitive than other dreams? What does this mean in regard to our response time?

3. Has God ever warned you in a dream? If so, how did your response affect what happened in your life?

4. What often accompanies a warning dream from God?

nine

Supernatural Impartation in Dreams

The apostle Paul in his letter to the Romans writes of his desire to visit with the church at Rome, that he might empower them through the grace of impartation that rested on his life:

> For God is my witness, whom I serve with my spirit in the gospel of His Son, that without ceasing I make mention of you always in my prayers, making request if, by some means, now at last I may find a way in the will of God to come to you. For I long to see you, that I may impart to you some spiritual gift, so that you may be established.
>
> Romans 1:9–11

The *Oxford Learner's Dictionary* defines the word *establish* as "to hold a position for long enough or succeed in something well enough to make people accept and respect you," "to make people accept a belief, claim, custom, etc.," and "to discover or prove the facts of a situation."[1] In the card game of bridge, to "establish" is a technique of playing off the high cards in a suit to ensure that the remaining cards in your hand are winners. The apostle Paul felt that if he could travel to Rome and impart to the saints, it would help establish them in their faith. Then they would be able to give greater proof to the resurrection of the Lord Jesus Christ and win in their mission of convincing the Romans of the truth of the Gospel message.

However, Paul wrote his letter to the Romans while stationed 600-plus miles away, in Corinth. The great distance between the two locations made it challenging for Paul to visit the church at Rome, that he might be able to impart to them some spiritual gift. We humans may be limited by distance, time, and space, but fortunately for us, God is not bound by these factors. God is able to impart to us spiritual graces and abilities no matter where we are. One of the ways He accomplishes this is in the dream realm.

The Lord Appears to a King

King Solomon was noted for his great wisdom and wealth. Scripture tells us, "Thus Solomon's wisdom excelled the wisdom of all the men of the East and all the wisdom of Egypt" (1 Kings 4:30). Although Solomon's leadership wisdom is what stands out the most, the Bible shares with us that his divine insight excelled in other areas of learning as well. Solomon wasn't just gifted in public administration, but it seems also in music, poetry, botany, zoology, and other disciplines: "He spoke three thousand proverbs, and his songs were one thousand and five. Also he spoke of trees, from the cedar tree of Lebanon even to the hyssop that springs out of the wall; he spoke also of animals, of birds, of creeping things, and of fish" (1 Kings 4:32–33).

The Bible shares with us the supernatural account of how Solomon obtained his gift of supernatural wisdom and understanding through a dream: "At Gibeon the LORD appeared to Solomon in a dream by night; and God said, 'Ask! What shall I give you?'" (1 Kings 3:5).

Solomon responds to the Lord's inquiry by asking, "Give to Your servant an understanding heart to judge Your people, that I may discern between good and evil" (verse 9).

God is so pleased with Solomon's magnanimity that He agrees to grant him even greater than what he asked for: "Behold, I have done according to your words; see, I have given you a wise and understanding heart, so that there has not been anyone like you before you, nor shall any like you arise after you" (verse 12). The Bible also reveals to us that "both riches and honor" are promised to Solomon in the dream (verse 13).

This biblical account reveals to us that the Lord is able to appear to His servants through dreams. Often, the Lord makes a personal appearance in a dream when He desires to communicate a special message or bestow a supernatural grace into our life. Solomon received a supernatural impartation of wisdom and understanding from the divine dream appearance he received from the Lord.

I Wanted to Be Slain

Years ago, I put a special prayer request before the Lord. I asked the Lord to let me be "slain in the Spirit." I had witnessed many individuals receiving prayer from the Lord's ministers that caused them to be touched by God in such a way that they would be "slain in the Spirit" or "fall under the power of God." Also, many people I had prayed for within my own ministry reported wonderful testimonies after experiencing this phenomenon. Several highly anointed ministers had laid hands on me in the past, but I had failed ever to be slain by the power of God through their prayers.

121

One night, God gave me a very realistic dream. The dream was set in a small gathering of believers in an outdoor tent meeting. I was one of the individuals standing in line, waiting to receive prayer from the minister working the altar. When the man of God approached me, I realized that it was the prophet and teacher John Paul Jackson. Immediately, when he laid hands on me, I was slain in the Spirit. As I lay on the ground under the power of God, I could feel the Holy Spirit's presence vibrating all over my body and permeating my inner being. It was such a wonderful and refreshing experience. John Paul Jackson leaned over and whispered into my ear a prophetic word about the ministry calling on my life. As he prophesied to me, it was as if my spirit man was translated into other localities and I was able to see two specific events that would take place in the future.

When I awoke, I was shocked that my experience had been a dream since it had felt so real. Suddenly, I noticed something, or rather someone, standing at my bedside. I glanced to my right and saw standing in my bedroom a tall, glowing angel with a large sword planted in the ground. Startled, I sprang up into a sitting position on my bed and had a few brief seconds to gaze upon the angel of the Lord. When the angel realized that I had seen him, he instantly changed into a large, bright, flaming ball of fire and suddenly disappeared.

That morning, I felt supercharged with faith and rejuvenated by the Spirit of God. For days afterward, I had the unusual sensation of being full of the Word of God. It was as if I had been intensively studying the Scriptures for many weeks. After that dream experience, I became more clear about the calling on my life and the decisions I should make within that season. That entire month, the prophetic anointing on my life was notably more acute and precise. I knew that God had allowed me to experience being slain in the dream, and He had also imparted a new level of grace into my life.

He Saw Her Face in His Dreams

In my early twenties, I had the privilege of sitting under the leadership of a pastor who had an amazing testimony of God's grace in his life. This man had served as a traveling evangelist, pastor, and advocate of divine healing. Before he was anointed as a preacher, he had a powerful encounter with God that forever changed his life and shaped his destiny.

In his twenties, this man fell ill. Before this time, he had felt perfectly well and was very active, like most young men his age. The day before falling ill, he had played sports with his friends and had felt perfectly well. But he had to be hospitalized because of his illness, and his life was soon rocked by terrible news from his doctors. The doctors announced to him that he had only a short time to live. They diagnosed him with several illnesses, more than one of them incurable. His diagnosis even included a brain tumor. The doctors had given up hope, the hospital chaplain was praying fear-filled prayers, and the believers he knew were telling him to prepare to meet his Maker.

At that low point, this young man began to study the Bible for himself while he was bedridden. One night, the Lord Jesus Christ walked into his hospital room and stood by his bed. The Lord spoke to him in an audible voice, saying, *You will not die, but live. I will send you all around the country and world to preach My Gospel.*

Soon doctors were baffled because all their medical tests reported that he was supernaturally healed of all his medical conditions! And soon after raising him up from his deathbed, God led him to join a local church and attend meetings each month conducted by the great Kathryn Kuhlman. This man shared later that many times when the doors would open to her services, the atmosphere would be electrifying. Healings, deliverances, and great miracles were the norm. He often sat in

123

one of the front rows and witnessed God's powerful ministry through this great woman of God in the 1970s.

It was sad news for him and so many others when God called Kathryn Kuhlman home to heaven. However, God was not done with her ministry in this man's life. Soon after her death, he started to have dreams with her in them. Before a big meeting, he would see her face in a dream or see her extending her hand toward him. Each time he would awaken from these dreams, he would feel that he had received some type of supernatural impartation as a result of sitting under and sowing into her ministry. He would share how whenever she would appear in his dreams, the signs, wonders, healings, and miracles would always be greater in his next few meetings. She never laid hands on him directly, but he indeed received something from her life and ministry.

God often will use the likeness of someone from the past in ministry, or will use a Bible character within a dream, to symbolize to a person what type of grace or anointing He is imparting to him or her. In this instance, Kathryn Kuhlman's appearance in this man's dreams represented an increase of the healing anointing on him.

No One Taught Him

God once gave me the privilege of working with the youth at a local church I attended. I would meet with the youth on alternating Sundays, and we would discuss the Word of God and the challenges in their lives. It's always a blessing to be part of speaking into the lives of young people as they grow in the knowledge of God.

During one of these youth sessions, the Lord had me share a prophetic vision with a young man. In the vision, I saw him playing a musical instrument in a church service. I asked if he had ever played this instrument before. He replied that he had not, but that recently God had given him a dream where he saw himself doing so.

The group decided to pray over this young man, that God would bless him supernaturally with the ability to play this instrument. I laid hands on him with the support of the group. We all asked God to stir up the gift that we believed was already given to him through the prophetic dream. He was very open to the prayer and lifted in his hands in agreement.

A few weeks later, I looked up to see him playing the instrument on the worship team during a church service! A few days after the prayer, he had decided to try his hand at playing it. To the surprise of his family, not to mention himself, he could suddenly play the instrument as skillfully as if he had spent years taking lessons. The church leaders caught wind of his newfound abilities and decided to allow him to play backup with their worship team. His skills only increased as he played and practiced his newfound gift.

This youth's story is one example of how God may impart a supernatural grace to an individual within the dream realm. We were all amazed that God had blessed him to play without training or any formal lessons. Although the divine ability to play the instrument supernaturally had been imparted to this young man, it took an act of faith to activate this ability. In a dream, God may show you yourself doing something great that you have never done before. Don't just dismiss the dream as insignificant. Instead, pray and exercise your faith to make the dream a reality. As we conclude this chapter, I want to make this prophetic decree over you:

Dear Father God, I decree now for this reader that the power of the Holy Spirit would descend into his or her life in a new and powerful way. Father, as this happens, please visit this person in the night hours with a supernatural encounter that will cause new talents, new abilities, and

125

new spiritual gifts to be released. Father, in Jesus' name I decree that as you bestow these new graces upon your child, he or she will achieve greater victories in life.

Summary

There are strategic times in our lives when God desires to impart special graces and spiritual gifts to us. We need these endowments in order to accomplish our divine assignments, help others, and fulfill the call of God upon our lives. The Holy Spirit will often manifest the impartation of these divine abilities through us in the dream realm. We should not take these dream encounters lightly, but rather exercise our faith to activate them in the "real world."

═══════ QUESTIONS FOR REFLECTION ═══════

1. Why is impartation from the Holy Spirit important? How does it help establish us in our faith?
2. What spiritual graces do you think are needed to help you in your God-given assignment? Ask God to show you more about this in a dream, and then be on the lookout for Him to answer your prayer.
3. Why might God allow a spiritually significant figure (like Kathryn Kuhlman) to appear in your dreams? Has this ever happened to you, and what was God communicating to you?
4. Have you ever experienced an impartation from God in a dream? What was it, and what effect has it had on your life?

ten

Decoding *Déjà Vu*

I can remember as a child grabbing a book off my bookshelf and suddenly having an unusual feeling that I had already lived this moment. I recall it being an eerie feeling because no one was in the house with me that particular day. This strange occurrence would happen many more times during my early years. It would always intrigue me when it happened, but leave me baffled. Several times, I would attempt to explain this occurrence to some of my friends and family, but most of them could not relate to it. The few who had similar experiences could only offer the story of their personal accounts, but not an explanation.

In my early teens, a friend of the family gifted me a set of books that he no longer desired. It was a series by Time-Life Books named MYSTERIES OF THE UNKNOWN. Each book in the collection would discuss and attempt to explain such supernatural phenomena as ghosts, psychic powers, space, ancient pyramids, UFOs, and life after death. In one of the books, I found a name for the strange occurrence that I had experienced at times as a youth. This was the first time I had ever read or heard of the term *déjà vu*!

While this Time-Life Book series was not based on Scripture, and while as a believer I don't agree with everything in it, the explanation I read of *déjà vu* at least reassured me that I was not alone. At least I knew that this supernatural occurrence was happening to more people than just me. The book offered its own explanations for the topic of *déjà vu*, but I never felt that the true answer was found within its pages. At that time, I had to settle for a half-answer. In my youthful state and spiritual immaturity, I was looking to this book series for understanding, but I don't recommend believers turn to secular sources for spiritual answers! The answer to my question would come years later, after asking the Holy Spirit and doing a careful study of Scripture.

Defining *Déjà Vu*

The term *déjà vu* originates from the French language and means "already seen." The term was first used by the French academic and philosopher Emile Boirac in 1876, and subsequently appeared in his literary work *L'Avenir des Sciences Psychiques*. *Merriam-Webster* defines *déjà vu* as "the illusion of remembering scenes and events when experienced for the first time," "a feeling that one has seen or heard something before," and "something overly or unpleasantly familiar."[1]

Have you ever walked into a store that you have never visited and had an overwhelming sense that you've been there before? Or maybe you meet a person for the first time, and when you shake hands it seems as if you've already met him or her? Perhaps you have heard of individuals seeking to purchase a house, and when they step into a particular home, it feels as if they've lived there before. These are some accounts of how *déjà vu* can and does happen.

Those who have experienced it know that *déjà vu* is more than just a sense of familiarity. Often, it is an overwhelming sensation accompanied by a feeling of supernatural awe. Also, it often seems as if time slows down or pauses for a moment. After the sensation of *déjà vu*, individuals often look around in their environment out of a sheer sense of shock. The experience rarely lasts for minutes at a time; often, it lasts only for a few seconds, and even more often, only for a split second. The person having a *déjà vu* experience feels as if he or she is reliving a real-world event.

Finding a Building

In 2011, my wife and I felt the call to plant a church. Planting a church is an endeavor that takes a lot of courage, wisdom, and faith. One of the most intimidating and daunting tasks was to find a meeting place for our new ministry plant. I knew the city that God had called us to pastor in, but I didn't know the specific location. Also, our financial resources were limited, and I wanted to avoid a facility that would drain our pockets.

One day in prayer I told the Lord, "I'm not going to worry about finding a meeting place. You called me to pastor. I did not call myself, so it's your job to show me the place for our church to meet." I didn't have the mental energy to drive around and try to figure it out by my own choice. As Proverbs 3:6 says, "In all your ways acknowledge Him, and He shall direct your paths." I recognized God as my guide and trusted Him to direct my path in this matter.

Two weeks later, I decided to attend a conference hosted by a fellow minister named Carolyn Philips. The conference was being held at the fellowship hall of a church that I had never visited. As soon as I stepped into the building—*BAM!*—it felt as if I had been in the building before. I knew that my spirit had caught a glimpse of this place in a dream months ago. I had come to attend the conference, but God gave me a witness through *déjà vu* that this was the building for my church to meet in.

On Monday, I contacted the pastors of the church and asked to meet with them to discuss renting their fellowship hall on Friday nights so we could begin holding church services. They agreed to meet with me, but also immediately accepted my request to use their facility. God gave them a yes! We had some powerful experiences at this meeting place, and it all started thanks to *déjà vu*.

The Red Sports Car

One day, I was speaking to a friend named Emil on the phone. When I walked into the kitchen, my mind suddenly reconnected to one of my past dreams involving the environment in that moment, the phone conversation, the kitchen setup, and something Emil specifically said. Immediately, I remembered this exact moment from the dream and knew instinctively that I should say to him, "You've been desiring a red Porsche. God has heard your prayer, and seeing your giving heart, He will bless you with it."

Emil was a person who always gave to the work of the Kingdom of God. He became elated at what I said and asked how I knew that he had been desiring a Porsche. I explained to him that the Holy Spirit had just brought back to my remembrance a dream that I had had several years ago, even before meeting him. In the dream, I had been on the phone, prophesying to a man, and now I knew that the man was Emil and that God would bless him with a red Porsche sports car.

Emil informed me that two years prior, he had several photos of Porsche cars printed out. He would look at them daily and release his faith that he would one day be blessed with one. The word from the Lord through me that he would be blessed with his dream vehicle encouraged him that God had not overlooked his prayer and that his act of faith was not in vain.

This story demonstrates how the Holy Spirit "will teach you all things, and bring to your remembrance all things" (John 14:26). The Holy Spirit is the one who gives us these *déjà vu* flashbacks from past dreams.

Hope Is Restored

One of the most pronounced accounts of *déjà vu* I can give you happened to me in 2013. One Sunday morning, as soon as I awoke, the Lord told me to go to a church service at a nearby church. It was a church I had driven past several times but had never attended. Jessica and I were welcomed there by very friendly greeters and were excited to see why God had sent us to this church. I felt that God must have a powerful prophetic word in store for us.

God had instructed me to attend the service, but at the time, I didn't feel adequately prepared for what happened at the end of it. The pastor stood up with tears on his face, stating that he had several announcements to make. The first announcement was that his youth pastors were leaving to start their own ministry. The youth pastors' parents were elders within this ministry, and they were also leaving to help their son and daughter-in-law plant their new church. Everyone was emotional because these all were beloved members who wouldn't be part of the fellowship anymore, and it was a big loss for the ministry.

The pastor followed the first announcement with a second, equally emotional one. He asked a couple to stand, who were also elders, and explained that they were leaving the church because they were being relocated by the U.S. Navy. The room was filled with intense emotions, tears, hugs, and a feeling of deep sorrow over all the transitions taking place within the ministry.

The pastor made one final announcement. The church was in deep debt and was unable to meet its monthly financial obligations. The loss of pillar members now compounded the issue because their leaving also meant more loss of income. The pastor and the members appeared broken, dejected, and defeated. My wife and I both became overwhelmed with emotion, and tears swelled up in our eyes. We grabbed each other's hands and squeezed tightly. It was a tense, emotional, and sad moment.

I wondered again, *Why has God sent me to this church?* I knew I had heard His voice, but this didn't make sense. I had walked into the church feeling good, and now felt downtrodden. I asked God in my heart, *Why did you bring me here?*

Suddenly, I had a Holy Spirit flashback. A glimpse of a portion from a past dream replayed in my mind. I had seen this church, these people, and this setting before, in a dream years ago. I instantly knew what to do. I exclaimed to my wife, "I know why God has sent me here!"

After the service, I ran up to the pastors and asked to meet with them in private. They were leery but agreed to meet in their office. I could sense that they were so overwhelmed from the emotional roller coaster of a service that they didn't really want to meet with first-time visitors, but they obliged my request. As Jessica and I sat across from them, I explained that God had spoken to me to attend their church, but that I hadn't understood why until a flashback from a God dream had played in my spirit. God told the children of Israel in Psalm 81:10, "I am the LORD your God, who brought you out of the land of Egypt; open your mouth wide, and I will fill it." I knew from the dream that I had seen myself sitting in this office, prophesying to these pastors. At the moment, I didn't know exactly what God desired for me to speak, but I felt that He had already downloaded the prophecy into my spirit within the previous dream, so I opened my mouth by faith and began to speak the word of the Lord to these pastors.

The pastor and his wife shook under the weight of the prophetic word, hugged each other, and praised God as tears flowed from their eyes. In the midst of turmoil and dismay, the Lord had sent a word of hope, purpose, and promise to give them encouragement and inspiration. A few years later, the pastor asked to meet with me. He shared how their circumstances had changed drastically, and how the church was now experiencing great church growth.

The Answer in Scripture

One night, I had a series of vivid and powerful dreams but became frustrated when I awoke and could only remember a few faint details. I prayed and asked God, *Why is it that although I'm intentional about recollecting all my dreams, there are some that are vivid during sleep but are only a faint memory when I wake up?*

I didn't expect the Lord to answer me so immediately, but He did. I hear Him say, *Some dreams are sealed!*

I then remembered from the book of Daniel that God had instructed the prophet Daniel to "shut up the words, and seal the book until the time of the end" (Daniel 12:4). I understood about the Bible prophecy being sealed, but God's answer about a dream being sealed wouldn't make sense to me until months later. However, the Word of God is so beautiful in that it can give a reader hope and encouragement, and build faith. Also, it is so multifaceted that it can also solve mysteries and bring answers to many of life's complex questions. One day while reading the book of Job, I came to understand one of the reasons why God speaks in dreams, a reason dreams are sometimes "sealed," and the mystery of *déjà vu*.

Let me explain. What is one of the main reasons God speaks in a dream? Think about this: God is always trying to get our attention. Rarely does He just come down from the sky and say,

"Hello there, John. I'm God, and I have a message for you." More often, He will speak to us within our spirit through His still, small voice, through an external sign, through the circumstances of life, through an impression, or through other people. Unfortunately, many of us are so busy with life or so distracted mentally that we miss God's first or second attempts to communicate with us. But look at what Job 33:14–16 tells us about God using a different way to communicate with us—through our dreams:

> For God may speak in one way, or in another, yet man does not perceive it. In a dream, in a vision of the night, when deep sleep falls upon men, while slumbering on their beds, then He opens the ears of men, and seals their instruction.

God has prepared a remedy for us, an alternate method of communication that often works when He is unable to get our attention during our waking hours. If He is unable to capture our attention while we are awake, He will speak to us through a dream while we sleep.

The New King James Version says in the verses we just read that "God may speak in one way, or in another," but the King James Version says that "God speaketh once, yea twice . . ." I believe both translations are accurate. God may speak more than once to gain our attention. Also, He may speak in more than one type of way to communicate with us. A dream is both another attempt and another method God uses to reach us.

We also see in these verses a reflection of the word God spoke to me months earlier: "He opens the ears of men, and seals their instruction." God had told me in an answer to prayer that often, dreams are "sealed." Job uses the word *seals*, but also explains what is being sealed: *instruction*. A sealed dream is one that is concealed. *Merriam-Webster* defines *conceal* as "to place out of sight" (keep hidden from view), and "to prevent disclosure or recognition of."[2] When God conceals a dream, it means a person's conscious mind won't remember the details of the dream, and the understanding of the dream is not disclosed. At a later date and time preset by God, fragments of the dream are brought into the person's conscious memory, or perhaps the dream in its entirety, often creating the ecstatic feeling of *déjà vu*.

In high school and college, I took some computer programming classes and learned about programming languages such as QBasic, Java, and C++. Programming languages contain defined rules of syntax and semantics that allow devices and computers to be programmed with code or specific instructions that produce specific outputs and cause the devices to behave a certain way. The end user of a computer sees the application, software, or graphical interface, but there is always code operating behind the scenes. Computer code often uses "IF-THEN" statements to cause something to happen at an appointed time, or based on certain criteria being present. God does something very similar with us. He gives us a dream. However, He may cause the dream to be like code downloaded into our spirit, which becomes useful at a future point in time.

The understanding of such a dream is "sealed" by God within our subconscious until the appointed time. When the time and circumstances for the concealed dream to happen in real life occur, then the Holy Spirit unseals the dream and we are already programmed for what to do and how to react in that moment. To the person experiencing this, it seems as if he or she has already lived through the event (in the form of *déjà vu*). In a way, the individual has experienced the life event before, albeit in the dream realm.

Concealed Dreams Help Guide Us

The multitude of methods God has created to communicate with His creation is amazing! We just saw how the ancient godly sage, Job, gave us further understanding of how God uses sealed dreams to guide, protect, and lead us. Yet there is still more to it. Job 33:17 goes on to reveal a specific reason why God may seal a dream: "in order to turn man from his deed."

In other words, God can use concealed dreams to help us make the right choices for crucial life decisions. One of the primary functions of the Holy Spirit is to empower us to live righteously and make wise and godly decisions in our daily affairs. One bad decision has been the ruin of many men and women. Wealthy investors have lost the bulk of their wealth from one bad business deal. God doesn't want us to suffer loss, but desires that we prosper. As the apostle John tells us, "Beloved, I pray that you may prosper in all things and be in health, just as your soul prospers" (3 John 2). God's communication with us through dreams can prompt us toward the right decisions.

Years ago, I was watching a reality TV show named *DEA* that featured Drug Enforcement Agency special agents conducting drug busts in Detroit, Michigan. In one of the episodes, the DEA agents arrested a woman who was selling heroin from her home. With tears in her eyes, her hands in handcuffs, and TV cameras pointed at her, she confessed that when the agents had raided her home, it was as if what was happening in real life was playing out a dream of hers from a week or so before. She had been feeling a strong prompting within the last week to stop selling drugs, but she hadn't heeded the warning. In fact, I believe she was experiencing *déjà vu* because God had already attempted to save her from imprisonment and turn her from an evil deed, just as Job 33:17 suggests.

Concealed Dreams Help Protect Us

We're not done with this chapter in Job yet. Look again at Job 33:17, and let's add verse 18 to it: "In order to turn man from his deed, and conceal pride from man, He keeps back his soul from the Pit, and his life from perishing by the sword."

As a loving, protective Father, God doesn't want to see His children walk in pride, destruction, or eternal damnation. In contrast, Satan is described as a thief in John 10:10: "The thief does not come except to steal, and to kill, and to destroy." Yet the work of Jesus in our lives always opposes the plans of Satan for us. Jesus tells us in the rest of that verse, "I have come that they may have life, and that they may have it more abundantly."

One of the ways Satan knows he can derail us is by causing our ego to be lifted up in pride. James 4:6 says, "God resists the proud, but gives grace to the humble." Proverbs 16:18 says, "Pride goes before destruction, and a haughty spirit before a fall." Since Satan knows that the Word of God cannot be broken, he loves to get individuals caught up in a haughty spirit of pride that will position them for loss, shame, and humiliation in their life. The great Babylonian king Nebuchadnezzar is a prime example of a person who was judged for his unrepentant pride and fell from grace. His arrogant boasting in his own abilities, and his dismissive attitude toward God having a hand in his influential, wealthy status caused a sentence of divine judgment to be issued against him from heaven:

All this came upon King Nebuchadnezzar. At the end of the twelve months he was walking about the royal palace of Babylon. The king spoke, saying, "Is not this great Babylon, that I have built for a royal dwelling by my mighty power and for the honor of my majesty?"

While the word was still in the king's mouth, a voice fell from heaven: "King Nebuchadnezzar, to you it is spoken: the kingdom has departed from you! And they shall drive you from men, and your dwelling shall be with the beasts of the field. They shall make you eat grass like oxen: and seven times shall pass over you, until you know that the Most High rules in the kingdom of men, and gives it to whomever He chooses."

Daniel 4:28–32

A further study of this account reveals that the king became insane and lived in the wilderness. His nails grew out like a bird's claws, and his hair covered his entire body. What a horrible sight to see! After an appointed time, however, Nebuchadnezzar was restored to his sane mind and kingship. I contend that God used a concealed dream at the appointed time to help bring him back to his correct senses and reveal his error of pride to him. This argument can be supported by the fact that he had once been a prolific dreamer who had powerful prophetic dreams that were concealed from him until the time of Daniel's revelation and interpretation (see Daniel chapters 2 and 4).

Many cases of *déjà vu* have been reported by individuals during crucial moments in their lives. For instance, many people have had such experiences right at the moment of a near-fatal vehicular accident. I have also read accounts of soldiers who, in the heat of battle, when a split-second decision had to be made, experienced *déjà vu* and somehow knew the right action to take. A wrong maneuver in the midst of combat could cost a soldier his or her life, or cost the lives of fellow soldiers. A right maneuver saves lives. This is the kind of thing God means in Job 33:18 by sealing an instruction and saving a life from perishing by the sword. God can use the dream realm to preprogram into our subconscious the right action to take, at the right crucial moment, that could save our life and the lives of others, and thwart the plan of Satan against us and/or others.

Summary

Déjà vu is not some psychic phenomenon that belongs to New Agers, but is a work of our heavenly Father, by His Holy Spirit, to instruct us. I propose that a better name for *déjà vu* should be "Holy Spirit flashbacks" or "Holy Spirit source code." After reading this chapter, you can throw the old worldly term *déjà vu* away and replace it with one that gives credit and glory to God. He divinely programs our subconscious, as a computer program would program the operating system of a computer. The next time you have a *déjà vu* experience, thank God, because He is working on your behalf. How great is our God!

QUESTIONS FOR REFLECTION

1. Have you ever experienced *déjà vu*? How has reading this chapter increased your understanding of this phenomenon?
2. Why does God choose to conceal the meaning of some dreams from us?
3. When was the last time God used a Holy Spirit flashback to protect or guide you? What happened (or didn't happen) as a result?
4. What action(s) will you take the next time you have a Holy Spirit flashback?

eleven

Dreams That Enlarge
Our Faith

God in His infinite wisdom has mastered how to build us up as individuals. Each one of us has been born into the "earth room" for a specific purpose, specific assignment, and specific era of time. Mordecai conveys this thought to his beloved niece, Esther, in Esther 4:14: "Yet who knows whether you have come to the kingdom for such a time as this?" Mordecai reasoned that Esther's ascension to the royal seat of queen, where she was privy to the king's chambers, was purposed by God, not by coincidence. Our God is not one of coincidence, but one who operates through divine intentionality and providence.

When God gives us a dream or vision, He does so with great intention and with attention to detail. The details within a dream matter. Also, the detail of when we have a dream matters; the season in our life and the affairs surrounding us at the time of a dream matter. One of the ways God uses dreams is to help shift us internally so we can fulfill His purposes and plans. These internal shifts could be a change in our thinking, our behavior, or our belief system, or an increase in our faith.

In this chapter, we will discuss the powerful potential of dreams to impact our souls in such a way as to cause personal growth and development. If we are going to manifest God's destiny within our lives, then we must be willing to accept new truths the Spirit of God presents to us. Also, we must be open to accept redirections that God may have for our lives. Dreams are a tool that help prepare us for these life changes.

Types of Learners

Educational theorists and professionals long ago discovered that every individual learns differently and at a different pace. It has been widely researched and accepted that there are different learning styles. Many experts define a learning style as an individual's preferred way to absorb, process, comprehend, and retain information. Understanding that different learning styles exist, educators have learned how to better create course materials and deliver learning content to maximize students' information retention.

Long before educators discovered that combining different learning styles was the best way to enhance learning environments, God already knew this secret. He actually operates this way in relation to us. The four main learning styles are *auditory*, *read/write*, *kinesthetic*, and *visual*. Let's examine how God uses all these methodologies to teach us His Word and His ways, and to convey to us His thoughts.

People who are *auditory* learners do best when content and information is delivered to them through spoken methods such as lectures, conversations, or preaching. These students learn best through hearing. Romans 10:14–15 lets us know that God uses the auditory method for individuals to be converted to Jesus Christ through the preaching of the Gospel: "How then shall they call on Him in who they have not believed? And how shall they believe in Him of whom they have not heard? And how shall they hear without a preacher?"

Your friend who has colored sticky notes posted everywhere in his or her house isn't crazy. This person may be a *read/write* learner. These types of learners absorb information and concepts best through notes, reading, or writings. This type of individual prefers reading a book to listening to a lecturer. God has made provision for these individuals through the *Logos*, or His written Word. Paul admonished his mentee Timothy in 2 Timothy 2:15 (KJV), "Study to show thyself approved unto God." How would Paul have studied? I believe he had books and writings to study from. Paul himself was very eager to have his written study material returned to him, as he told Timothy: "Bring the cloak that I left with Carpus at Troas when you come— and the books, especially the parchments" (2 Timothy 4:13). Paul seems to have been a *read/write* learner. This theory about him is further evidenced by the fact that he wrote three quarters of the New Testament.

People who are *kinesthetic* or tactile learners are often called "hands-on learners." They learn best by doing, and through touch and motor activity. This is the person who would prefer on-the-job training over reading a manual or attending a seminar. Tactile learners demonstrate their proficiency in comprehending new ideas through completing projects. God has given us the wonderful opportunity to be tactile learners within His Kingdom through participation and serving within the local church. The local church is a microexpression of the Body of Christ at large. Through ministry projects, assignments, and serving in the local church, we learn how to put the Word into action within our lives.

The other learning style is called *visual*. Visual or visionary learners learn best through graphic presentations such as pictures, diagrams, graphs, charts, and 3D models. It can be said that *visual* learners are greater at retaining knowledge through what they see. These types of learners are often very intuitive, right-brained, and concept driven, in contrast to *read/write* learners, who are often very left-brained and logic driven. God ministers to our spirit and subconscious in a visionary style through visions and dreams. Understanding this will be very important in grasping how God uses dreams as a visionary tool to imprint information and new concepts about ourselves and the world around us into our beings.

Dreams can be used by God to warn us, instruct us, and impart graces, as we have seen in earlier chapters. But He also uses dreams to help us expand in faith, learn about His ways, and grow as individuals. You don't necessarily have to be a visual learner for God to use dreams in these ways with you; He can use dreams with anyone, no matter what a person's learning style. Yet it does help if you understand how He can work within your specific learning style.

I Have a Stomachache

When God started to wrestle with me about accepting my call to ministry, I wasn't exactly happy. I reasoned with God for days, giving many reasons why I was not a good choice for ministry. Also, while in prayer, I shared with Him my many reservations about being selected as a preacher. One of my main arguments was that I was not a good public speaker. In the past, I had always been somewhat nervous when asked to speak in front of crowds. As a kid, I would avoid situations that required standing before an audience. Being part of plays, the choir, or anything of that likeness was totally out of the question for me. I remember as the president of my fifth-grade class, I was asked to say the pledge of allegiance and give a short speech to the student body. Conveniently that day I had a stomachache and had to leave school

144

early. I chickened out! Later, the thought of having to speak in front of people, even if it was for God, gave me the same stomachache.

Eventually, I surrendered to the call of God and said yes to His beckoning. However, there still existed anxiety about having to pray or speak publicly. God sent several prophetic vessels to encourage me that God's call and hand was upon me and that I should continue to move forward with ministry. Before I fully understood the prophetic ministry, it would amaze me how individuals who had never met me before could discern the call of God on my life and speak with precision about things that I had prayed to Him about in private. God greatly used these individuals to help build my faith and confidence.

In addition to prophetic people speaking into my life, God used prophetic dreams to encourage me. One year, I had several dreams where I would see myself standing in front of a crowd of people, and I would be praying or sharing the Gospel. Each time God would give me a dream, He would show me standing with greater boldness and authority before a different crowd of people, sharing His heart with them. At the time, some of these dreams were mind-blowing and unbelievable. Many of those dreams have since come to pass in real life.

Each time God would give me dreams of speaking in public, my self-confidence would increase. Eventually, it became natural to stand before people and speak in the name of the Lord, not only with confidence, but with an absolute assurance that God would manifest in miraculous ways for His people. Proverbs 23:7 says, "For as he [a man or woman] thinks in his heart, so is he." God's dreams penetrate deep into our subconscious, impact our thinking, and change how we feel about ourselves and the circumstances surrounding our lives. God dreams have the ability to help you and me see ourslves the way God sees us. God always sees us as more capable than we see ourselves.

Joseph's Great Ambitions—or Not?

A study of Joseph, who was noted as a dreamer of dreams and a person gifted with the ability to interpret dreams, reveals much to us. Joseph's first dream encounter is recorded in Genesis 37. An analysis of this particular dream helps us understand how God uses dreams to increase our faith and prepare us for destiny:

> Now Joseph had a dream, and he told it to his brothers; and they hated him even more. So he said to them, "Please hear this dream which I have dreamed: There we were, binding sheaves in the field. Then behold, my sheaf arose and also stood upright; and indeed your sheaves stood all around and bowed down to my sheaf."
>
> Genesis 37:5–7

In Hebraic culture, as in most ancient cultures, it was a cultural norm and expectancy for the eldest male sibling to assume leadership within a tribe, clan, or family lineage. Joseph had ten older brothers who would all have been offended by his dream and the very suggestion that they would be his servants, or that he would outrank them in life. His brothers' responses to his dreams reveal this fact: "And his brothers said to him, 'Shall you indeed reign over us? Or shall you indeed have dominion over us?' So they hated him even more for his dreams and for his words" (verse 8).

Joseph's brothers were offended at the notion that he would be greater than they were. Also, there existed the internal family politics that resulted from all of the brothers being born to Jacob (Joseph's father) by mothers different than Joseph and Benjamin's mother. It was well-known that the mother of these two boys, Rachel, was the wife Jacob loved the most. This certainly led to some form of jealousy and resentment among his other wives and their children.

146

Joseph's brothers were not happy with his first dream, and probably were even less elated about his second dream:

> Then he dreamed still another dream and told it to his brothers, and said, "Look, I have dreamed another dream. And this time, the sun, the moon, and the eleven stars bowed down to me."
> So he told it to his father and his brothers; and his father rebuked him and said to him, "What is this dream that you have dreamed? Shall your mother and I and your brothers indeed come to bow down to the earth before you?"
>
> Genesis 37:9–10

This second dream Joseph shared with his siblings and father was even more of an affront to them. Even Jacob seemed perturbed by the dream's implications. His response conveys that he may have found his son's dreams ludicrous. The family seemed to have held the consensus that Joseph was speaking nonsense and maybe was touched with a bit of egotism.

If Joseph's siblings possessed divine insight into the plans and purposes of God, they would have discerned that Joseph was not an overly ambitious and self-important lad, but that God was using these dreams to position him for greatness. These dreams early in Joseph's life programmed him to believe that he would one day be a great leader. God used the power of prophetic dreams to deconstruct the limitations that may have been placed on Joseph's mind by the social norms of his day. Remember that because he was the next-to-youngest son, it would not have been normal for him to expect to be ruler over his brethren. God had to impart the possibility of this into his mind.

Afterward, in every situation Joseph later found himself in, he excelled as a leader, even when it was beyond normalcy. For instance, it was abnormal for a bondservant to be prosperous and to run the affairs of an Egyptian officer's household. Yet in Genesis 39:2 we read, "The LORD was with Joseph, and he was a successful man; and he was in the house of his master the Egyptian."

It was also abnormal for a prisoner to be placed in charge of a prison house and the prisoners within it. But God had already shown Joseph through a dream that he would be in abnormal circumstances of authority and influence. Genesis 39:20–22 tells us,

> Then Joseph's master took him and put him into the prison, a place where the king's prisoners were confined. And he was there in the prison. But the LORD was with Joseph and showed him mercy, and He gave him favor in the sight of the keeper of the prison. And the keeper of the prison committed to Joseph's hand all the prisoners who were in the prison; whatever they did there, it was his doing.

When Joseph became second to Pharaoh in the governance of Egypt as a result of his gift of interpreting dreams, his own dreams would soon manifest into reality. All the brothers who rejected him came to him desperate for assistance. Their very livelihood, and that of their families, depended on Joseph's benevolence during a time of great regional famine. Joseph could have sought vengeance against his victimizer relatives, but instead God used the dreams from his youth to instruct him at a very critical juncture: "So Joseph recognized his brothers, but they did not recognize him. Then Joseph remembered the dreams which he had dreamed about them . . ." (Genesis 42:8–9).

Remembering his dreams helped Joseph know that this was the very moment that God had predestined—the moment when he would stand as a ruler in Egypt and therefore be in a position to help his brethren. He was able to forgive them for their betrayal and see things from God's perspective. Joseph reassured his brothers that it was God who had allowed their betrayal and had used it for His long-term plans: "And God sent me before you to preserve a posterity for you in the earth, and to save your lives by a great deliverance" (Genesis 45:7). God had used dreams to build Joseph's faith that he would one day be a deliverer for his entire bloodline!

A Lesson Learned

There is a great lesson to learn from the life of Joseph the dreamer. Not every dream from God is meant to be shared with everyone. Some of the prophetic dreams God gives you have the 007 anointing—they are for your eyes only! Often, before God releases a dream that is meant to challenge your faith or reveal some deep truth, He has already spoken things to your spirit and used life lessons to prepare you to receive new truths. Others may not yet have received the same preparation.

During a supernatural commission from the Lord, the prophet Isaiah was instructed that he would encounter the dilemma of receiving revelations that were beyond the comprehension level of much of his audience. In Isaiah 6:8–10 the prophet wrote,

> Also I heard the voice of the Lord, saying:
> "Whom shall I send, and who will go for Us?"
> Then I said, "Here am I! Send me."
> And He said, "Go, and tell this people:
> 'Keep on hearing, but do not understand; keep on seeing, but do not perceive.'
> "Make the heart of this people dull, and their ears heavy, and shut their eyes; lest they see with their eyes, and hear with their ears, and understand with their heart, and return and be healed."

God was telling Isaiah that the potential for the children of Israel to be redeemed and healed existed, but that there would be the challenge of overcoming their lack of understanding. When you go to share certain revelations with others, it likewise may be difficult for them to receive. This is because God may have prepared you to receive these truths, but did not prepare those around you. Joseph found himself in this predicament with his brothers. He believed what God was revealing, but it was difficult for his older brothers to accept it as truth. God was dealing with Joseph, but not with them. Maybe Joseph initially felt his revelation would bring their admiration, but instead it provoked the hearers to jealousy and hatred.

Years ago while working for a marketing company, I shared with a co-worker a revelation about a future world event that God had shown me would come to pass. I had seen it in a dream the night before. This co-worker frowned at me, set his coffee down, and sarcastically asked, "Do you have a brain tumor?"

Mixed emotions flooded my heart. I didn't know if I should burst out laughing or become angry with him for his inappropriate response. He followed up with, "Maybe you should get checked out!"

I was offended by his response, and I attempted to argue with him that I indeed had heard from God about this future event. Needless to say, this was the last time I would share a prophetic revelation with him. This co-worker's response was one of ridicule.

Other times, I have shared dreams with other ministers of the Gospel concerning my destiny or something that God desired to do with our ministry. I expected a shared excitement on their part, but often was met with an undertone of envy. These life experiences have taught me that some dreams are meant to stretch us, prepare us for greater, increase our faith, and enlarge our expectation with the things of God, but are not meant to be shared liberally with others.

Convincing My Wife

The Lord revealed in 2005, during a prayer meeting, that I would eventually move to Atlanta, Georgia, and that it would be the headquarters for the ministry God would give me. At that time, I had never been to Atlanta and had no desire even to visit the city. Over the next few years, several friends and relatives moved to Atlanta, yet still I had no desire to visit. Although I believed the word of the Lord and received it as the truth, I made no effort to tour the city. I left the matter in God's hand and timing.

A decade passed since the first word from the Lord had come that I would end up living in Atlanta. By then, I had traveled to Atlanta several times for ministry engagements and other events. The idea of moving there was slowly growing on me. One day, I shared with my wife that I felt we should pursue moving to Georgia. She already knew about the word that God had given me about a relocation to Atlanta. It had come before we had even met. She was not excited about it, however, and had no desire to leave Virginia.

One morning, Jessica shared a dream with me that God had given her. In the dream someone asked her, "Where do you live?"

My wife responded, "We live between Virginia and Georgia."

Jessica felt as if God was using this dream to prepare her to be more open to the idea of moving to Georgia. After her dream, I invited her to accompany me during my next ministry assignment in the Atlanta, Georgia, region. I felt that actually setting her feet on the land and experiencing the environment would build her desire and faith to move.

I was wrong! We traveled to Georgia together for my next assignment, but the venue for the speaking engagement was in an area of Metro Atlanta that was dimly lit, somewhat dilapidated, and lacked newer amenities. In addition, the area around our hotel was sketchy. Jessica returned to Virginia discouraged about any potential move to Georgia. I prayed about it, knowing that God would somehow turn her heart again so that His will could be fulfilled.

When the Lord desires something for your life, He knows how to change your heart. Psalm 37:4 says, "Delight yourself also in the LORD, and He shall give you the desires of your heart." Many have mistakenly interpreted this verse to mean that whatever we desire in life, God will grant our request. But God is not our genie in a bottle. What this verse means is that as we grow in the knowledge of God, draw closer to Him, and surrender to His plans, He changes our inner desires. We begin to desire what He wills for our lives. This is what it means to truly delight oneself in the Lord.

The Lord went to work on my wife. As she spent more and more time with God, He gave her more dreams concerning Georgia. God wanted to encourage her that the move to Georgia was from Him and that it would be for our betterment. Jessica had one dream where she saw us walking the streets of a beautiful neighborhood in Georgia. In another dream, she saw us hosting a powerful ministry event at a place of worship in Georgia. Other dreams followed in which she would always see our family in Georgia, doing things that were enjoyable and pleasant.

A few years later, God had changed Jessica's mind after several prophetic dreams and a few more trips to Georgia. The woman who once had been dead set against moving from Virginia was now gung ho about it. I remember several days seeing Jessica frustrated because things had not fallen into place yet for us to move. I increased my time seeking the Lord about the relocation, knowing He would give us a sign concerning the perfect timing.

One night, Jessica had a dream that we were loading a U-Haul truck with a lot of our personal belongings. In the dream, before we drove off to leave Virginia, my aunt stood on our sidewalk and told us farewell. We knew from this dream that it was now time to move. God used this dream and others to encourage us and boost our faith. One of our friends even had a dream about the property we would purchase on a cul-de-sac, with trees surrounding our home in a peaceful neighborhood. She had no idea that her dream matched the exact property we were considering buying. Several other people started having dreams that we were leaving Virginia. Our faith was now skyrocketing!

The move happened so fast. In a matter of weeks, we were approved for a home loan, found a home to purchase, and planned an interstate move. Amazingly, we never physically saw the property until after we closed on the home. Our faith and confidence were so high that we acquired the house after only viewing it online, touring it virtually, and trusting the reliability of our real estate agent. All the circumstances surrounding the move fell into place perfectly. God exceeded our expectations. Several of the dreams God had given us previously were now manifesting in real life.

God used dreams to change Jessica's mind and heart about moving to Atlanta. He also used dreams to give us supernatural faith to move within an unprecedented time frame and under some unusual circumstances. We moved during the height of the Covid epidemic, when many were gripped with fear and economic uncertainty. God provided supernaturally every step of the way, and prophetic dreams were instrumental in aligning our hearts with His desire so that we walked in His faith and wisdom.

Summary

The apostle Paul prayed for the believers in Ephesus, that "the eyes of your heart may be enlightened" (Ephesians 1:18 NIV). Dreams are one of the modes God uses to open our spiritual eyes and illuminate our minds to what He desires to do in us and for us. God dreams often remove spiritual blinders that cause doubt and unbelief within us. Such dreams have the supernatural ability to cause us to be laden with faith and to see life from a new, fresh perspective. The Holy Spirit uses dreams as prophetic building blocks for our future. Expect God to enlarge and strengthen you through faith-filled dreams.

QUESTIONS FOR REFLECTION

1. What learning style do you identify with most—*auditory*, *read/write*, *kinesthetic*, or *visual*? In what way do you think this has affected how you receive from God?

2. God uses dreams as part of the visual learning style, yet why don't you necessarily have to be a visual learner to hear from Him in this way?

3. What is one reason that you shouldn't always share your prophetic dreams with everyone?

4. Has God shown you yourself in a dream doing anything in the future that you never thought you would be able to do? If so, how does this encourage your faith?

Twenty Questions
& Answers about
Supernatural Dreams

1. Why do some people never dream? Also, why do some people, who once dreamed often, stop dreaming or dream less frequently?

I have met only a few individuals who have said that they never had a dream. I believe that some of them may have actually experienced dreams, but for some reason they had an inability to recall them. It also seems that people who are more aware and conscious of God dream more readily and remember their dreams more easily.

For those people whose dream life has decreased or come to a standstill, I suggest rereading chapter 2 in this book, "Activate Your Dream Life Now." Applying this chapter's instructions should help give your dream life from God a boost. Also, I have noticed that even the most profound dreamers have cycles of dreams, and seasons when they may dream more or less.

2. How often should an individual expect to receive a supernatural dream from God? Is it normal for God to speak to someone in dreams every day, or is it less frequent?

Within my own life, I have peaks and valleys of dreams and revelations. Some seasons, I may have four or five supernatural dreams per week. Other times, I may have one or two dreams every three to four weeks. There are a number of variables involved in how frequently a person dreams. These variables include the person's environment, prayer life, stress level, openness to God, diet, and much more. The important thing is not how much you dream, but that you make yourself available to God so He can speak to you. After we exercise wisdom in the variables we can control that affect sleeping and dreaming, the rest is up to God.

3. Why do some dreams feel more real than others?

I believe the weightiness of a dream causes it to feel more or less real. Most dreams feel like basic dreams. However, there are some dreams that have more of a real feel to them. A person may awaken feeling as if he or she has been engaged in some real activity, has traveled to another location, or in reality has reacted with other individuals.

Many of these dreams that feel lifelike are very lucid in nature. In a lucid dream, you are aware that you are dreaming and aware of every activity taking place. Also, it seems as though your mind has more control over the decisions and interactions taking place within the dream. Dreams that involve spiritual warfare or an encounter with God often have this type of lucid attribute.

I believe Solomon's dream where the Lord appeared to him was one of these lucid or lifelike dreams. The Lord appeared to Solomon and inquired about his heart's desire: "At Gibeon the LORD appeared to Solomon in a dream by night; and God said, 'Ask! What shall I give you?'" (1 Kings 3:5). I believe Solomon's own subconscious was able to engage and reply to the Lord within the dream. This dream was recorded in Scripture for our learning, as it surely was realistic enough to have been indelibly embedded into Solomon's memory.

4. Are some dreams from God more important than others?

I believe every attempt God makes to speak to us has significance. There are certain dreams, visions, and revelations that we should take more seriously due to the content and impression they make on our soul. God has a way of highlighting for us the communications from Him that carry greater significance.

For example, one time I was praying about God's provision for a certain project. The deadline was quickly approaching, and I was a bit stressed. God gave me a dream with actor Dennis Haysbert in it, the "Allstate guy," saying to me, "You're in good hands!" I felt it was God's way of telling me that He had my back and would provide help regarding this matter. When I awoke, it was if those words were still ringing in my ears. Later in the day, when I went to watch TV, the first thing that came on the screen was a commercial featuring Haysbert as the Allstate guy, and he ended it with the words, "You're in good hands!" God used this to hit home the message that He was on my side.

5. How can I better understand the timing of things God shows me in my dreams? What are some clues that something might be close to happening?

Understanding the timing of God is one of the most challenging yet rewarding undertakings. Many revelations are so vivid and intense that they seem as if they are about to happen immediately. In fact, many of the early saints felt that the visions and dreams they received of Christ's Second Coming and the millennial reign of Christ were very imminent. The apostle Peter himself said in 1 Peter 4:7, "But the end of all things is at hand." He may have felt that all of Scripture would be fulfilled in his lifetime. That was not the case, however, as God's timing is not man's timing.

Dr. Bill Hamon addresses this topic in his book *Prophets and Personal Prophecy: God's Prophetic Voice for Today.* He comments, "Through both biblical study and personal experience, I have discovered that God's time terminology differs considerably from ours. Though He never seems to be in a hurry, He is always on time. But He often seems to take longer than we think he should."[1]

6. **What does it mean if I keep having recurring dreams about being in the childhood home I grew up in?**

Recurring dreams about a childhood home are not uncommon. Often, this means there are unresolved issues from one's childhood that need to be addressed and brought before God. Psychologists report that for the majority of us, our core personality is formed by age seven. Dreams that deal with our childhood often highlight these core traits of our being. Many adults' negative beliefs, attitudes, expectations, and anxieties root back to childhood trauma or happenings.

Also, it's not uncommon for a person to dream about being at a residence that was important during that individual's childhood, such as the house of a grandparent, aunt, or uncle. This is especially true if life-altering events took place at the property the person is dreaming of. Many individuals equate life-forming moments to a relative's home, more so than to their own childhood home. A supernatural dream may highlight this factor and the need for some type of deliverance associated with that family member or the time frame during which the dreamer is frequenting that property in his or her dreams.

God may give an individual a recurring dream about being in a childhood home to expose a familiar spirit He desires to free a person from. In 1 Samuel 28, King Saul desired to communicate with the deceased prophet Saul, and this story reveals to us how mediums and psychics would use familiar spirits. The Bible outlaws the practice of consorting with familiar spirits to communicate with the dead or to supernaturally gain information (see Leviticus 19:26; Deuteronomy 18:10–11). For more information on this subject, read my book *Discerning of Spirits: 7 Dimensions of Revelation.*

Also, there are familiar spirits that are attached to people's bloodlines. The Latin root word for the word *familiar* is *familia,* which means a family or household. These spirits gain access to family lineages through the past sins of our ancestors and help enforce generational curses within families (see Leviticus 26:14–39; Deuteronomy 28:15–68). They are often the cause for cycles of failure, sickness, instability, and certain sins that repeat themselves within certain families. When God gives a supernatural dream about a childhood home, it could be the catalyst for breaking a generational stronghold of demonic curses and familiar spirits off a person's life and lineage.

7. **Please explain the meaning of a specific color or colors being highlighted within a dream.**

Colors are a common way that God may communicate a message to you within a dream. He may use colors that have a specific meaning or importance to you. For instance, I know one young lady whose favorite color is turquoise. When God would give her dreams about hearing and/or answering her prayers, He would often send a dream in a turquoise setting.

A color within one person's dream may mean something different than it does in the next person's dream. The context, activity, and dialogue within a dream are other factors we need to take into account, along with whatever colors might be highlighted. Some colors, however, have common themes when they are emphasized. Green, for instance, often may deal with healing. Silver or gold may deal with prosperity. Purple often deals with influence, favor, and authority.

8. **Should I share a dream with a person who appears in or is involved in the dream?**

This can be tricky and requires the Holy Spirit's leading. Joseph shared his dreams with his brothers and it backfired (see Genesis 37). They hated him all the more for sharing his dreams, even though his supernatural dreams were from God. Being a youth who maybe was not yet spiritually mature, Joseph may have shared the dreams prematurely. There have been times that I have shared dreams with individuals, much to my own chagrin.

If God reveals through a dream that a person may be facing an imminent threat or harm that may come to him or her, it's important that we share the dream almost immediately. Sadly, you may find that many people don't take a dream message from God that you deliver to them as seriously or urgently as they should. You may need to inquire of God concerning the proper wisdom and tact about how to deliver such messages.

There are times that a person appears in your dream not because God is giving you a warning for them, but rather a warning about them. God desires to protect His children. Several times in my life, God has shown me the true intentions and motives of individuals through a dream. Rarely would God have me share such nighttime revelations with these persons; rather, He desired for me to disassociate with them.

Some dreams that involve another person are God's way of letting you know in advance that there will be a connection between you and that person. Several times, God has shown me interacting with a person (often a minister of the Gospel) in a dream. Years later, God would supernaturally connect me with that individual. God used the dream to let me know the importance and divine purpose of the relationship in advance.

9. Do I have to be knowledgeable of the Bible to understand the dreams God gives me?

Understanding a dream from God does not always require a knowledge of the Bible. God speaks to a person in ways and languages that he or she can understand. Jesus often taught parables that were agrarian in nature because He knew that the common people could understand kingdom principles that were analogous to farming. As we grow in spiritual maturity, however, God expects more from us and often begins to communicate with us in more advanced ways. Over time, therefore, a greater knowledge of the Word of God not only becomes highly instrumental in dream interpretation, but also in preparing one's heart to receive from God.

10. What is the difference between a dream and a vision in the night?

Visions and dreams are both exhilarating and re-velatory. They both can give us insight into the mind of Christ and the mysteries of God. A vision is very similar to a dream, except a person is awake when receiving a vision. Also, a person may have different types of visions—an inner vision, an open vision, or a trance vision. But in every vision scenario, the person is awake when receiving revelation. Visions tend to have more of an immediate impact on a person because the senses are actively involved since the person is awake.

A night vision happens when someone is awakened in the night and sees a vision. A night vision can also occur before a person falls asleep at night. One night, my wife had a very vivid dream that awakened her. After Jessica was fully awake, she had three insightful back-to-back night visions.

I have had similar experiences where some nights I have had both dreams and night visions. This is rare, but it does happen. It seems to have been the case with King Nebuchadnezzar, who experienced both in Daniel 4:5: "I saw a dream which made me afraid, and the thoughts on my bed and the visions of my head troubled me."

11. I have heard preachers warn against eating food offered to you within a dream. Is this warning something I should take seriously? Why should I avoid eating food served to me in a dream?

Yes, one must be careful if offered food within a dream. Many of these types of dreams are lucid, where your subconscious is able to make a decision whether to reject or accept the food. Unfortunately, there are workers of iniquity who engage in witchcraft practices, and they issue spiritual attacks through appearing in people's dreams and persuading them to eat spiritual food. This happens often in places steeped in black magic, such as in West Africa and Haiti. After eating the food, the unsuspecting person may fall ill, be overcome with anxiety, or start experiencing unusual symptoms.

Jessica and I knew of a woman who visited a village in another country to see some relatives. While in this village, she began to pray against the generational spirits of idolatry and wickedness attached to the family and the land they lived upon. Right before she returned to the United States, she had a dream in which some beings appeared to her and offered her some food to eat. She asked them in the dream, "Are you angels?"

They replied, "Yes. Now eat!"

Her inner spirit accepted their answer, and she proceeded to eat the food they presented to her. The very next day, the most unusual thing happened. Parts of her body viciously swelled up, her face became distorted on one side, and she became seriously ill. As she sought the Lord, He revealed to her that yes, the entities were angels, but that she had not asked the right question. They were angels indeed, but were fallen angels summoned by forces of darkness. God told her that she should have asked, "Are you holy angels of God?" or "Are you holy angels of the Lord Jesus Christ?" The unholy, demonic entities had duped her.

This woman called me and shared this revelation. We prayed together, pleading the blood of Jesus Christ and exercising our authority through the name of Jesus.

163

Within a few short days, the vicious attack broke and she was back to normal. The enemy tried to use deception, but the Lord prevailed in her life. (For further reference, see Luke 10:19; 1 Corinthians 12:3; 15:27; 2 Corinthians 11:14.)

12. **If the Lord shows me in a dream something "bad" that will happen, how do I know if it's something that can be reversed or canceled through prayer?**

Sometimes it can be difficult to discern if God is showing us something to prepare us for what will happen, or if He is enlisting us for intercession. If God shows me something negative, contrary to His will, or a work of the enemy, I often instantly pray and take authority over whatever was revealed. Also, there is a burden of prayer that accompanies supernatural dreams where God is desirous that we intercede through prayer.

There have been times I have dreamed about some type of catastrophic event. I went to prayer to reverse the matter, but realized that God was revealing a divine judgment to me. He was showing me what would happen, that I might stand as a prophetic witness of the actions He would take on the earth in response to wickedness and disobedience. God revealed to Abraham His plans to judge the cities of Sodom and Gomorrah (see Genesis 18:17–33). Abraham was able to lessen the judgment, but nevertheless, divine judgment did fall.

In some dreams, God shows us things that may not be pleasant for us to see, but He is showing us what will happen in the future. As Amos 3:7 tells us, "Surely the Lord GOD does nothing, unless He reveals His secret to His servants the prophets." For instance, a person may dream of a loved one passing away, and they go immediately to prayer to cancel the event from happening but feel unable to cancel the matter. God hasn't give the dream to invoke intercession in these cases, but rather is preparing the person's heart so he or she is not caught off guard by the sudden passing of the loved one.

13. **How do I know if God is speaking to me about my past, present, or future within a dream?**

   Looking for clues within a dream will help you determine if God is speaking to your past, present, or future. If people and places from your past appear in your dream, it's a good indicator that God is speaking to your past.

   If people, places, and things from your present appear in your dream, it's an indicator that God is speaking to your current season. Also, if the dream speaks to present anxieties or challenges within your life, that's another clue that a dream is for your present season.

   Futuristic dreams seem to be the easiest to discern, as you will often see yourself, your children, or close associates as older. Also, seeing yourself with people and in places that you have never seen before often indicates a futuristic dream.

14. **Most of my dreams consist of fruits and gardens. I see certain fruits and I know they are a symbol for something, but there may not be a biblical reference to them. How can I interpret what these things mean?**

   Fruits and gardens are usually a good sign within dreams. I believe that God may be speaking by using these elements because they have a personal meaning to you. God will often speak in a way that has special significance to us. If you are a gardener or a person with a green thumb, it would make sense for God to speak to you in this kind of language.

165

A search for the fruits mentioned in the Bible should be a starting point or reference with such dreams. For fruits not found in the Bible, ask yourself what the fruits you are seeing in the dream mean in the natural. For instance, there is a well-known saying that "an apple a day keeps the doctor away." Therefore, apples in a dream may speak to health and healing. Pomegranates are known for having many seeds. Seeing a pomegranate in a dream could mean that you are a person with many gifts and talents. Two Christian books that I recommend for further reference on understanding dream symbolism are Apostle Jane Hamon's *Dreams and Visions: Understanding and Interpreting God's Messages to You*, and Dr. Sandie Freed's *Understanding Your Dreams: How to Unlock the Meaning of God's Messages*.

15. **Does everyone possess the ability to interpret dreams? I often dream, but I have difficulty interpreting my dreams.**

   I believe there is a special gift of the interpretation of dreams. However, I believe with enough practice, insight, and dependence on God, anyone can learn to interpret dreams. The gift of prophecy is similar. There are individuals who are especially gifted with it, but the Bible also says in 1 Corinthians 14:31, "For you can all prophesy one by one, that all may learn and all may be encouraged." In a similar way, while dream interpretation can be a special gift, I believe receiving and understanding dreams from God is for everyone.

16. **What if I miss or misunderstand the message God is trying to communicate to me within a dream?**

   I'm sure this has happened to all of us dreamers. God gives us a message through a dream, but we are either too busy with life or not discerning enough to ascertain His communication. Yet God is a gracious and merciful God. If we are open to Him, He will make other attempts to communicate with us. He may speak again through a dream or through some other mode, such as a vision, the voice of the Holy Spirit, a supernatural sign, or a third party.

17. **Is there a reason that all my dreams are in black and white? I don't dream in color like other individuals who have shared their dreams with me.**

    The few individuals I have encountered who dream in black and white have two things in common: they seem to be more seasoned persons (above the age of 65), and they grew up watching black-and-white television during their childhood. I believe God uses the black-and-white imagery because it may capture the attention of these people's subconscious minds who grew up during a time when television was in black and white.

18. **I keep seeing certain number sequences in my dreams. What does that mean? For instance, I always see the number 444 in my dreams.**

    Number sequences from God are an adventure in themselves. I have known individuals who, both in real life and in dreams, always seem to encounter certain number sequences, such as 111, 333, or 444. A careful study of what each number represents in the Bible will help you interpret what God is saying for you. God revealed to me that 444 is a number that deals with possessing divine inheritance. There were four rivers that watered the Garden of Eden (dealing with land and territory); there are four gospels; and believers are told to go to the four corners of the earth in Christ's Great Commission (representing God's inheritance of souls).

19. Should I be concerned if I keep seeing a deceased relative within my dreams?

Yes, I would be very concerned. I would bring the matter before God in prayer. Seeing a deceased relative repeatedly in a dream could mean the presence of a familiar spirit. (Please refer to question 6 for more information on this topic.)

There are times, however, when God may use the imagery of a deceased relative to communicate a message of hope to someone in a dream, especially when the person is experiencing a season of heavy trauma or grief. Yet we must be prayerful and cautious about desiring or attempting to speak to deceased relatives or people in dreams, or through any other mode. Again, seeing a deceased relative repeatedly in a dream could mean the presence of a familiar spirit.

I advise that people be prayerful and discerning concerning these types of dreams, asking God (and if necessary, mature Christian leaders) for personal insight.

20. How much weight can the average believer place on his or her dreams?

This is a difficult question to answer because, depending on people's spiritual maturity and keenness, their dream lives may be less or more prophetic. Also, a person's ability to understand his or her dreams factors heavily into how much weight a person should place on dreams. In his book *Take Another Look at Guidance*, author Bob Mumford suggests that we should only give about 30 percent weight to our dreams.

My general rule of thumb is that if you are unsure whether or not a dream is from God, I suggest placing that dream on the proverbial shelf, praying, and waiting to see if God speaks about the dream. If you are sure a dream is from God, you should place great weight on it. However, my personal practice is that a direct word from the Lord or the voice of the Holy Spirit trumps a dream within my own life.

Acknowledgments

This book is dedicated to my wife, Jessica, and our four beautiful children who, in between asking me to kick the soccer ball, play LEGO, and engage in other games with them, afforded me the time to work on this project!

Also, I would like to especially thank my core intercession team with Destiny 4 the Nations, Inc., who labor tirelessly and selflessly in prayer for our family, ministry, and the will of God. These are my real unsung heroes!

In addition, special thanks to Ms. Lisa Johnson for her prayers and words of encouragement for us to move forward in the glory of God. Also, to Ms. Silina Edmonds, who has been super consistent in her support and love for us.

Many others I would like to thank include the Means family, Pastors Brett and Mary Smith, our Arise Texas Team, our Bermuda ministry family, Ms. Nadeia Smith, Dr. Shirene Anderson, Revelation Church, and Pastors Henry and Donyale Wells.

Finally, I would like to thank many international prophetic voices for their support and encouragement, including Apostle Chuck Pierce, Dr. R. Abraham in India, Apostle Jane Hamon, Bishop Brian Keith Williams, and Apostle Prince and Prophetess Glenda Jackson.

Notes

Introduction Dreams Are Treasure Chests

1. *News from Google* Announcement, "Larry Page's University of Michigan Commencement Address," *Google*, May 2, 2009, http://googlepress.blogspot.com/2009/05/larry-pages-university-of-michigan.html.

Chapter 1 How to Remember Your Dreams

1. *Merriam-Webster*, s.v. "expect," accessed March 2023, https://www.merriam-webster.com/dictionary/expect.
2. Bible Hub, s.v. "5046.teleios," https://biblehub.com/greek/5046.htm.

Chapter 3 What Happens When We Sleep

1. Ana Sandoiu, "Sleep Deprivation May Cause Dehydration," *Medical NewsToday*, November 7, 2018, https://www.medicalnewstoday.com/articles/323595.

Chapter 4 Dream but Discern

1. "Brain Basics: Understanding Sleep," National Institutes of Health (NIH), accessed February 2023, https://www.ninds.nih.gov/health-information/public-education/brain-basics/brain-basics-understanding-sleep#:.
2. *Merriam-Webster*, s.v. "imagination," accessed March 2023, https://www.merriam-webster.com/dictionary/imagination.

Chapter 5 Those Bad Dreams

1. "Nightmares," American Academy of Sleep Medicine (AASM), October 2020, https://sleepeducation.org/sleep-disorders/nightmares/.

2. *Merriam-Webster*, s.v. "nightmare," accessed 2023, https://www.merr iam-webster.com/dictionary/nightmare.
3. *Merriam-Webster*, s.v. "nightmare."
4. Merrill Perlman, "The History of 'Nightmare': The 'Mare' Has Many Meanings," *Columbia Journalism Review*, January 20, 2015, https://archives .cjr.org/language_corner/the_history_of_nightmare.php.
5. Dictionary.com, s.v. "phobia," accessed 2023, https://www.dictionary .com/browse/phobia.
6. Kendra Cherry, "List of Phobias: Common Phobias from A to Z," *VeryWell Mind*, February 13, 2023, https://www.verywellmind.com/list-of -phobias-2795453.

Chapter 6 The God Kind of Dreams

1. Mahesh Chavda, *The Hidden Power of Prayer and Fasting* (Shippens-burg, PA: Destiny Image, 1998), 16.
2. Adapted from Bishop Bennet Aboagye and Apostle Dr. Gina Aboagye, *At the Appointed Time: The Kairos Moment* (Los Angeles: Book Writing Inc., 2018), xi.

Chapter 7 The Dream Compass

1. *Merriam-Webster*, s.v. "compass," accessed 2023, https://www.merriam -webster.com/dictionary/compass.

Chapter 8 God's Alarm in the Night

1. Samuel Oakford, "Burundi Is 'Going to Hell' Says US Ambassador to United Nations," *Vice News*, December 14, 2015, https://www.vice.com /en/article/ev9574/burundi-is-going-to-hell-says-us-ambassador-to-united -nations.

Chapter 9 Supernatural Impartation in Dreams

1. *Oxford Learner's Dictionary*, s.v. "establish," accessed 2023, https://www .oxfordlearnersdictionaries.com/us/definition/english/establish?q=establish.

Chapter 10 Decoding *Déjà Vu*

1. *Merriam-Webster*, s.v. "*déjà vu*," accessed 2023, https://www.merriam -webster.com/dictionary/déjà%20vu.
2. *Merriam-Webster*, s.v. "conceal," accessed 2023, https://www.merriam -webster.com/dictionary/conceal.

Twenty Questions & Answers about Supernatural Dreams

1. Dr. Bill Hamon, *Prophets and Personal Prophecy: God's Prophetic Voice Today* (Shippensburg, PA: Destiny Image, 1987), 118.

Demontae Edmonds travels globally as an apostolic ambassador, sharing the Good News of Jesus Christ. Multitudes around the world have experienced his ministry through television, radio, and conferences. The ministry God has given him is earmarked by the glory of God and the presence of the Holy Spirit. God has performed many deliverances, healings, and miracles in Demontae's ministry, including the blind seeing, the deaf hearing, the lame walking, metal disappearing from bodies, limbs growing, supernatural weight loss, and many other miracles. In a single meeting, Demontae has had a dozen partially or fully blind people see by the healing power of Jesus Christ. Many of these supernatural testimonies have been recorded on video.

Demontae's heart is to equip and empower today's and tomorrow's leaders. He has ministered to as many as three thousand or more pastors and ministry leaders in one setting, and God has used him as a voice to accurately deliver major prophetic words or messages for churches and secular leaders for over a dozen nations.

Demontae is the overseer of The Father's House, an apostolic network partnering with and covering churches and ministries throughout the United States and abroad. He has also been the special guest on many regional, national, and international TV and radio broadcasts. In 2022, God led Demontae and his wife to rebrand Freedom 4 the Nations—the ministry he founded in 2015—to Destiny 4 the Nations, Inc., to better reflect the mission of this ministry to bring individuals, communities, and nations into their God-given destiny.

Demontae is also the author of *Grab Hold of Your Miracle: 10 Keys to Receiving Supernatural Miracles*, *Discerning of Spirits: 7 Dimensions of Revelation*, *The Supernatural Gift of Faith: Unlocking New Realms of Prophetic Power*, and *How to Win in Life & Never Lose: A 30 Day Devotional of Proverbial Wisdom*.

When not involved in ministry activities or empowering others, Demontae enjoys traveling, dining, and playing with his children. He is proudly the husband of Jessica, and they have been happily married for more than fourteen years. They reside in Atlanta, Georgia, with their four lovely children. The entire family serves and worships the Lord Jesus Christ together. For more information on Demontae and his ministry:

@DemontaeTV

@DemontaeTV

@DemontaeTV

www.f4nations.com